BRIDGING THE GAP

BRIDGING THE GAP

Perspectives on Nationally
Competitive Scholarships

THE NATIONAL ASSOCIATION OF
FELLOWSHIPS ADVISORS

Edited by Suzanne McCray and Dana Kuchem

THE UNIVERSITY OF ARKANSAS PRESS
FAYETTEVILLE
2019

Contents

III International Awards

IV On the Profession

Foreword

In July 2017, the National Association of Fellowships Advisors (NAFA) held its ninth biennial conference in Philadelphia, Pennsylvania. As with every biennial conference that preceded it, the Philly conference was the largest that NAFA had ever held with over 470 attendees, a 14 percent increase from the attendance at the 2015 conference in Oakland, California. The conference theme, "Mind the Gap," was intended to be both a reference to the warnings that many Americans fail to heed when boarding trains in England and an invitation for our members to consider, explore, and discuss the various "gaps" in our professional practice. What groups of students might we be disregarding? What programs had we overlooked? What resources had we not created to help our students succeed? In other words, NAFA members (who are, by nature, self-reflective) were asked to investigate what they had not yet investigated.

This task may seem daunting for new advisors, who already have plenty to consider. I can recall my first NAFA conference—Louisville, Kentucky, in 2005. I had just been offered my first fellowships advising job; I had not yet seen my office, met my boss, figured out my benefits, or even purchased a parking pass. I also barely had any context for the deluge of odd names I overheard while lurking in the elegantly appointed hallways of the Brown Hotel: Udall, Gates, Goldwater, Pickering, Gilman, Fulbright. Everyone around me seemed to be communicating in an obscure patois, and I felt completely out of my element, a stranger in a strange land. I wanted to get back in the car, go back to my old office, and start working on my syllabus for the next term of sophomore "Intro to Literature." I felt that a mistake had been made.

For new advisors, who are typically defined in NAFA circles as anyone with less than one year of experience (we expect our children to grow up quickly), everything is a "gap." Every single program has its own byzantine application system, puzzling criteria, and unwritten codes. Furthermore, most new advisors are also learning to adjust to a completely new campus or academic unit and cannot even enjoy the benefit of helpful colleagues or mentors. If the academy were a swimming pool, fellowships advising would be in the deepest end of it. More often than not, NAFAns jump (or are pushed) in with both feet.

As NAFA approaches its twentieth anniversary, however, a significant number of our members are what might safely be described as "veterans." For fellowships advisors who have been swimming in this end of the pool for over five years, the gaps in knowledge are less about deadlines, criteria, and acceptable font sizes and more about cultivating a fellowships culture on campus, strategies for building alliances, or insights on long-term professional development in a field that has no consistent career ladder. Much like the heads of the fabled Hydra, the "gaps" in fellowships advising knowledge seemingly multiply after being resolved. Finding a way to meet the needs of both new and experienced advisors is one of the great challenges in designing our programming. Thankfully, collaboration is a core ethos of NAFA, and our colleagues once again outdid themselves in Philadelphia. Our organization is also unusual in that we bring together all stakeholders—fellowships providers and fellowships advisors—to articulate "best practices" that not only serve one another, but also serve our students, our institutions, and (most importantly) the greater good. Indeed, I am assured that NAFA remains true to its central mission of promoting the full potential of fellowship candidates through the application process and fostering the growth and professionalization of fellowships advising.

The impossibility of mastery is simultaneously the most attractive quality and the primary frustration of our work. As I have progressed in my career, I cannot help but note that it never gets any easier. Every year, new programs arrive and old ones fade away. Generations of students, university administrators, and foundation representatives come and go. We add new programs, create new seminars, build new websites, write new guides, forge new partnerships. Every gap in the calendar gets filled with new deadlines, new meetings, new ideas, new initiatives, new events. Every year, new gaps open and old ones close. This book represents various efforts to bridge some of the gaps in our knowledge and should serve as an excellent resource for advisors both new and old. As someone who is now a veteran among the veterans, I am perpetually amazed and impressed by the high quality of my colleagues' work. Every biennium, the quality of the insight improves, the profession grows, and the professional networks strengthen.

Kyle Mox
NAFA President, 2017–2019
Arizona State University

Acknowledgments

This volume includes many essays that resulted from presentations delivered at the ninth biennial National Association of Fellowships Advisors (NAFA) conference, held in July 2017 in Philadelphia, Pennsylvania. An event of this size requires hard work from many talented people. The conference and this volume would not have been possible without Dana Kuchem (University of Richmond), who was the president of NAFA at the time of the conference and had established high standards for organization and excellence. Kyle Mox (Arizona State University) was vice president in the two years leading up to the conference; in this role, he served as chair of the conference planning committee and led the efforts to organize this national event—coordinating speakers, calling for papers, organizing sessions, negotiating logistics, and countless other responsibilities.

The lion's share of the credit, however, goes to the conference planning committee, which included Andrus Ashoo (University of Virginia), Brian Davidson (Claremont McKenna College), Kurt Davies (New York University), Kristin Janka (Michigan State University), Marynel Ryan Van Zee (Carleton College), and Sue Sharp (IIE). Special thanks to local chair Meredith Wooten (who was at Drexel University at the time of the conference and is now at University of Pennsylvania), who provided substantial support and access. Elizabeth Colucci (University at Buffalo) spearheaded the New Advisors' Workshop, while Megan Friddle (Emory University) and Lora Seery (IIE) organized the Fulbright Reading Session. Laura Sells (Arizona State University), our conference planning administrator, kept the committees on track, and John Richardson (University of Louisville) continued to be an invaluable asset for NAFA, working first as treasurer (2001–2013), and then as NAFA's first employee (2014–present). Other board members who contributed to the effort who have not been named elsewhere but who deserve recognition, include NAFA executive officers Brian Souders (University of Maryland, Baltimore County), Jeff Wing

(Virginia Commonwealth University), and Lauren Tuckley (Georgetown University) for their important contributions to the site selection and planning.

Scholarship- and fellowship-awarding foundations and organizations are key members of NAFA, sharing their expertise with advisors at conferences, during campus visits, and in the proceedings. Special thanks to NAFA board member Sue Sharp (IIE) and to all the foundation members who participated in the structured foundation interviews or "chat" sessions. Representatives who gave generously of their time included Derrick Bolton (Knight-Hennessy Scholarship), Carolina Chavez (Mitchell Scholarship), Jane Curlin (Udall Scholarship), Mary Denyer (Marshall Scholarship), Robert Garris (Schwarzman Scholarship), Elliot Gerson (Rhodes Scholarship), Stefanie Gruber-Silva (DAAD), Craig Harwood (Soros Fellowship), John Holden (Yenching Academy Scholarship), Bo Knutson (Critical Language Scholarship), Lewis Larson (James Madison Fellowship), Lauren Marquez-Viso (Rotary Scholarship), John Mateja (Goldwater Scholarship), Gisele Muller-Parker (NSF GRFP), Christine O'Brien (Ford Foundation), Patricia Scroggs (Rangel Fellowship), Lora Seery (IIE and Fulbright Program), Jaclyn Sheridan (Pickering Fellowship), Jim Smith (Gates Cambridge Scholarship), Kelsey Ullom (Gilman Scholarship), Tara Yglesias and Andrew Rich (Truman Scholarship), and Katherine Young (Hertz Fellowship).

The NAFA publications committee also deserves thanks for its support of this project, especially Brian Davidson (Claremont McKenna College), who also administered the 2019 *NAFA Survey of the Profession*. Thanks also go to Lauren Tuckley (Georgetown University), chair of the publications and technology committee, and members Laura Clippard (Middle Tennessee State University), Valeria Hymas (Baruch College, CUNY), Suzanne McCray (University of Arkansas), Liz Romig (American University), Kelly Thornburg (University of Iowa), and John Richardson (University of Louisville). Brad Lutes (University of Arkansas) richly deserves recognition as well for his work on the survey.

Thanks go to the University of Richmond administration, including Stephanie Dupaul (vice president of enrollment management) and Ronald Crutcher (president), for supporting this work, as well as the staff at the Office of Scholars and Fellowships. The Ohio State University also deserves thanks for its support of this conference. Thanks go as well to

Joseph Steinmetz (chancellor) and Jim Coleman (provost and senior vice chancellor for academic affairs) of the University of Arkansas for their ongoing support. Special thanks also to the Division of Enrollment Services at the University of Arkansas and the staff of the Office of Nationally Competitive Awards in particular. Jonathan Langley (associate director) and Emily Wright (associate director) provided excellent proofreading support. Liz Lester (production manager) at the University of Arkansas Press designed the striking cover. The continuing support of Michael Miller (dean), Ketevan Mamiseishvili (associate dean), and Michael Hevel (department chair of Rehabilitation, Human Resources and Communication Disorders) in the College of Education and Health Professions has been greatly appreciated. And of course, this publication would not be possible without the excellent work of the University of Arkansas Press: Mike Bieker (director), David Scott Cunningham (editor in chief), and Melissa King (marketing director).

Introduction

This year marks the twentieth anniversary of *Truman and Marshall Scholarships: Breaking the Code,* a fellowships advisor workshop held in Fayetteville, Arkansas, in the summer of 1999. The conference focused mainly on two major scholarships but included information about others as well. That foray into advisor and foundation information sharing on multiple scholarships sparked the creation of the National Association of Fellowships Advisors (NAFA), officially launched a year later in Chicago by a group of fifteen advisors, most of whom had attended *Breaking the Code.* That first conference was about understanding the basics, comparing notes, reaching out directly to foundation members, *breaking their codes.* After twenty years, some of the same discussions are still relevant as scholarships change goals and requirements, as new awards like the Schwarzman have been added to the opportunities available to students, as advisors develop new competitive award programs for the first time on their campuses, or as new advisors accept a fellowships advising role (approximately one-third of advisors who are members of NAFA have held such a job less than three years). Breaking the code can still seem overwhelming to many. NAFA conferences and books like this one have helped provide what can seem to those just starting out as insider information, but what is actually an effort to create a framework for providing support for exceptional students seeking transformational opportunities to further their academic goals and their professional and personal aspirations.

Those early days have been followed by deeper examinations of the work that both advisors and foundations do. Different conferences, as well as the resulting proceedings, have focused at least to some extent on different recurring themes: the value of the process (*Beyond Winning*), service (*Serving Students and the Public Good*), leadership (*Leading the Way*), access (*All In*), holistic approaches to serving students (*All Before Them*), and increasing the scope of awards (*Roads Less Traveled*). At the 2017 NAFA conference held in Philadelphia, attendees at the "Mind the Gap"–themed event were charged with considering "the gaps that exist both in our advising practices and in the broader contexts that shape them, as well as how [advisors and foundations] might bridge or eliminate them." And it is the bridging of such gaps that the essays in this volume seek to do.

The essays included in *Bridging the Gap: Perspectives on Nationally Competitive Scholarships* are for the most part (though not exclusively) a product of presentations, roundtable discussions, and percolating ideas that were generated for or at the 2017 conference. The collection is divided into four parts. The first, "Serving Students," expands the ways advisors can best support students through the creation of new learning opportunities, by reducing or eliminating bias in the recruitment and selection process, by giving students support and (equally important) space to continue to develop a sense of identity, and finally by allowing students to sink or swim on their own accord. The second, "Best Practices for Advisors and Advising Offices," offers pragmatic advice for advisors on a range of topics including the specific practices of recognizing and addressing gender bias in letters of recommendation, setting up effective selection panels, establishing strategic plans that can drive an office forward, and understanding how graduate students search for opportunities and what that means for their advisors. Part III focuses on international awards—how to develop a general campus environment that supports international awards and how to establish a student culture willing to take the leap to explore another culture intellectually, academically, and personally. Part IV includes the biennial *Survey of the Profession* to allow directors and staff of individual advising offices to understand the landscape of advising work being conducted across the country.

Karen Weber and Ben Rayder in the volume's opening essay, "Early Research as a Pathway for Nationally Competitive Awards," make the case for fellowships advising offices to become engaged in active learning programs like undergraduate research, study abroad, and service learning. The authors examine various high-impact practices—a phrase that is currently much discussed in higher education circles—including the actual act of supporting students as they apply for nationally competitive awards. They conclude that perhaps the most effective way to bond students with faculty is through research. To that end, the University of Houston's Honors College created the Houston Early Research Experience (HERE) that serves all students on the campus, not just honors students. The program recruits and then prepares freshmen and sophomores for future research. Students participate in a two-week workshop in May to learn research fundamentals. The essay details the goals, the student benefits, and the successes of the program. It also makes a persuasive case that such programs can effectively inform students about and guide them to offices of merit awards, which can in turn assist students, who are already on their way in developing strong faculty connections and a research profile, in choosing and competing more successfully for award opportunities that best fit their long-term goals.

Chapter 2 focuses on the Morris K. and Stewart L. Udall Scholarship. Authors Suzanne McCray, Jane Morris, and Paula Randler are all experienced Udall Scholarship reviewers, and Randler is a former Udall Scholar herself who also served as a program manager of the scholarship for several years. This essay provides reviewer perspectives on how applications are read, what leadership means within the Udall Scholarship context, and how the well-known "Udall factor" is applied. One of the most salient points is that leadership can be viewed very differently by different scholarship programs and that advisors should be careful to review the individual foundation values (like Udall's "civility, integrity, and consensus").

Authors Richelle Bernazzoli, Joanna Dickert, Anne Moore, and Jason Kelly Roberts examine authentic student motivation and drive in chapter 3's "Excellent Sheep or Passionate Weirdos? Fellowships and Fellowships Advising as Vehicles for Self-Authorship." The article begins with an analysis of the perceived and actual purposes of higher education and relies heavily (and takes part of its name from) a controversial but interesting book by William Deresiewicz, *Excellent Sheep: The Miseducation of the American Elite and the Way to a Meaningful Life*. Deresiewicz eschews the sheep and celebrates the weirdos. As chapter 3's title promises, the authors of this article also look at how students fall into traps of what is expected rather than examining what it is they actually hope to learn, to accomplish, and to be. The article meshes theory with practice and ends with examples of two students who, after relevant experience and self-reflection, decide on a path that seems more appropriate to their goals. They may or may not be fully developed "passionate weirdos," but they do seem to be headed in a direction that feels designed by and right for them.

The last essay in this section (chapter 4) is from Tara Yglesias. Once again Yglesias does not disappoint in her article, "You Sank My Fellowship: The 'Near Miss' Truman Application." Yglesias has written many articles on the Truman application process for various proceedings on topics ranging from what constitutes leadership to Truman reviewers, to how students should think about developing a postgraduate studies plan, to surviving the Truman interview. All are written with an inimitable flair. "You Sank My Fellowship" is a lively look at why students may not move forward to an interview from the written application review process. Readers of this essay should not be misled by the jaunty prose or the game framework (literally games like Scattergories, Apples to Apples, Connect Four, Chutes and Ladders) that Yglesias employs. Hers is a serious look at why dedicated, talented, and even amazing students are sometimes (indeed all too often) not included as Truman finalists, and it is an easy step to apply these assessments to a broader set of opportunities. Advisors who may have a comprehensive view of the talented students on their own campus are less likely to have that comprehensive view of the applicants that come from across the country. Here students and advisors are likely to take comfort. That there is simply a subjective aspect of choosing scholars that cannot be avoided is less appealing, but may benefit an advisor's students on some occasions if not on others.

Part II lays out practical guides both for creating offices and for establishing advisor practices that work efficiently and effectively to serve students. Chapter 5's "Gender and the Characterization of Leadership in Recommendations for Nationally Competitive Awards" is an interesting dive into gender bias found in letters of recommendation for students applying for nationally competitive scholarships especially in connection with a student's leadership development and skill sets. Paula Warrick, ably assisted by Ketevan Mamiseishvili, Andy Rich, Patricia Scroggs, and Jane Curlin (the latter three foundation heads), provides a brief literature review of gender differences in letters of recommendation and then maps those studies to real examples of bias found in letters received by scholarship foundations. The article explores what may constitute bias or stereotyping. As in chapter 2, the article also reinforces the notion that a definition of leadership is relative to the scholarship in question, and that advisors would benefit from keeping an individual award's selection criteria in mind while drafting letters of endorsement or nomination or when advising faculty on the tenets of an individual program. Creating a campus culture that acknowledges and seeks to address bias can be challenging. This article provides concrete ways an institution can move forward productively in that process.

In their essay "Best Practices for Scholarship Advisors in Managing the Room Where it Happens," Doug Cutchins and Greg Llacer provide a step-by-step approach to what can be another challenging process: selecting campus nominees for competitive awards. In yet another aspect of the process, being fully informed about the selection criteria is a key starting point. Cutchins and Llacer then address the strategic composition of faculty committees. Once committees are set, they suggest how to effectively engage members in what can be a demanding process. This article provides an excellent guide for new advisors with its detailed plans for everything from room and time scheduling to the role of the advisor during the meeting. But experienced advisors will also benefit from the nuanced look at committee ethics and the how-to on mediating debates that can arise over individual students. All who organize such committees or who run offices will find the tips on how to "avoid or manage conflict, promote collegiality, and handle difficult personalities" helpful.

Dacia Charlesworth, in chapter 7, tackles a tough topic—the dreaded strategic plan. Most experienced advisors have survived extensive work on strategic plans (see the *Survey of the Profession* in Part IV) only to find they have been shelved in an upper administrative office somewhere to no effect and likely cringe whenever such a planning process is suggested by campus administrators. Charlesworth acknowledges this up front in her article "Strategic Planning for Fellowships Offices: Minimizing Challenges, Identifying Stakeholders, and Optimizing Benefits" and writes persuasively on why such planning is important and can be beneficial to an office even if the recommendations put forward are only reviewed and adopted by that office. She also very helpfully outlines the process specifically for a fellowships office, complete with strategic questions and analyses to begin the review, ways to map office goals with a university's mission and guiding principle statements, appropriate timelines for completing the project, and steps to turn objectives into measurable outcomes that benefit a variety of constituents—the university, colleges and departments, the office itself, and students being served.

In chapter 8 (the final essay in Part II), Teresa Delcorso-Ellmann shares results from research conducted on the Rutgers University campus about how graduate students search for scholarships. Rutgers provides students with a home-grown search tool called GradFund. Behind the scenes, administrators of the tool can see how students approach their searches. What Delcorso-Ellmann and her team learned was interesting— graduate students are more likely to search according to their research activity rather than their discipline or graduate program, and they rarely read past the first page of results, leaving possible (and perhaps more appropriate) opportunities unexplored. Many advisors in NAFA provide services to both undergraduate and graduate students, but a growing number of advisors only serve graduate students. A separate NAFA listserv was created recently to support this population, and studies like the one provided in Delcorso-Ellmann's "How Do Graduate Students Search for Fellowships and Grants? Why Knowing Matters" are likely to expand going forward. The research in this article provides another avenue for understanding how to provide students with key information that will help them pursue awards that best match their discipline, research interests, and time to degree, and so is well worth duplicating on a home campus. Knowing what they are missing can be as important as knowing what they have found for both graduate and undergraduate students.

Part III focuses on international students, first through developing a campus culture of support for students applying for international *awards,* followed by a look at how to support international *students* who are applying for awards. Laura Clippard's "Fulbright 101: Developing a Fulbright Campus Culture" posits that developing a campus culture that supports international scholarships like the Fulbright first means understanding the culture that currently exists and exploring which offices might be supportive partners if they knew more about the whys and hows of a particular scholarship. Establishing campus partners, co-opting faculty, and celebrating student success and those who have supported them can help transform a campus from one unaware of international scholarship programs to one that is working as a unit to recruit for and support students through the application process. Most universities agree in principle with Senator Fulbright that "educational exchange can turn nations into people, contributing as no other form of communication can to the humanizing on international relations." But the pragmatics of making this idea a part of campus culture takes effort, and Clippard outlines how an awards office can make it happen.

Charlotte Evans's "NAFA Gone International: Support Global Applicants through the Fellowships Process" that follows in the next chapter (10) is a companion piece that provides a case study of advising non-U.S. students on a particular campus abroad (Yale, NUS) and the lessons gleaned from those efforts. Evans points to cultural differences that advisors in the United States should be alert to when advising international students on nationally competitive awards. Advisors do not want to make blanket assumptions, but knowing that different students from different cultures may approach topics like leadership and service in very different ways is essential. What is being straightforward to one student can seem like bragging or impudence to another. Evans provides suggestions based on experiences with her own students that will certainly be helpful to a broader audience of advisors.

Ending this collection of essays with one on cultural competence is appropriate, given the work foundations and advisors do and the students both groups support. Foundations create funding and spaces for scholars to expand their understanding of what is "other," to embrace new challenges while meeting new people, and to think globally as they prepare for meaningful careers that have the potential to bring change to many different corners of the world. Advisors seek to connect the right student with the right opportunity. Self-reflection on biases and internal motivations, and what it means to be an authentic (self-authored) individual, is important for students, advisors, and reviewers alike. Whether the student's focus is research, creating public policy, starting an NGO, or teaching English in other lands, diplomacy skills will be required. Those who support these students also share their values with them—sometimes intentionally, sometimes not. Taking a lesson from one of NAFA's own members, we would all do well to strive for civility and integrity as we aim when possible for consensus.

Part I

Serving Students

1

Early Research Program as a Pathway for Nationally Competitive Scholarships

KAREN WEBER AND BEN RAYDER

Karen Weber is assistant dean of Co-curricular Programs at the University of Houston's honors college. In this capacity, she supports faculty and staff in developing, implementing, and assessing experiential learning opportunities. She oversees a grant from the Andrew W. Mellon Foundation that supports an undergraduate research and graduate school preparation program for students in the humanities. Weber is also director of the Honors e-Portfolio program. In this capacity, she teaches an e-portfolio course, lectures to students on developing professional websites, and advises faculty on using e-portfolios for assessment. Weber's doctorate is in educational learning, design, and technology. She conducts research on learning and career e-portfolios, as well as high-impact practices in higher education. Before arriving at the University of Houston in 2005, Weber worked in the nationally competitive scholarships office at the University of Illinois at Chicago. She has been a member of the National Association of Fellowships Advisors (NAFA) since 2003, serving on *the Nominations and Elections Committee in 2012 and assisting with print and web materials for the organization.*

Ben Rayder *is director for National Fellowships and Major Awards and instructional assistant professor in the honors college at the University of Houston. As part of his responsibilities, he creates awareness for external fellowship opportunities and helps candidates with the development of application materials. Rayder also oversees the Houston Scholars, a competitive program that prepares high-achieving freshman and sophomore students to apply for major awards. Rayder's doctorate is in comparative politics with a focus on extremism and German politics. Before arriving at the University of Houston in 2017, Rayder worked as the assistant director in the fellowships office at Drexel University. He has been a NAFA member since 2016.*

Administrators and faculty members in higher education are constantly inundated with pedagogies, practices, and trends to adopt. Recent movements include the need to incorporate technology into the classroom, a heightened emphasis on assessment, and the encouragement of interdisciplinary work. (All good practices to be sure, but a lot for one to manage.) Another gold standard on college campuses currently is providing opportunities for ***active learning***. These practices might be labeled as experiential learning, engaged learning, problem-based learning, project-based learning, cocurriculars, case studies, or any other number of pedagogical terminologies that involve learning through doing. Fortunately, this effort has been mostly positive. Universities across the country are dedicating substantial resources to activities our scholarship candidates typically take advantage of, such as common first-year courses, internships, and capstone experiences.

Active Learning in Higher Education

The active learning movement stems largely from George Kuh's research on the effectiveness of high-impact practices, affectionately referred to as HIPs.[1,2] Kuh advocates for colleges and universities to offer HIPs to students in order to enhance student success and engagement. HIPs are credited with strengthening "deep learning, practical competence, general education, and personal and social development."[3] They might also be one way to address inequities within higher education; HIPs can enhance the learning for students from many backgrounds.[4] Kuh's eleven designated HIPs range from activities such as collaborative assignments, writing intensive courses, and e-portfolios to undergraduate research, service learning, and study abroad.

HIPs for Fellowships Advisors

How do HIPs affect the students we counsel as scholarship advisors? Certainly, these high-impact activities shape our students' learning and guide them in their intellectual and professional journeys. The experiences promote both deep and integrative learning.[5] They enable students to take ownership of their academic trajectory and often guide them in their future pursuits upon graduation. An argument could be made that the intrinsic process of applying for nationally competitive scholarships should be considered a high-impact practice due to its extensive degree of engagement and student and faculty collaboration.[6] A competitive application can take countless hours of time and effort for applicants. The application process compels students to think critically about their curricular and cocurricular activities, and then through this reflective process, they are better able to share their narrative with their audience and crystalize their future plans. The process also has the added benefit of acquainting students with crucial application components, such as writing a personal statement, asking for references, and possibly interviewing. These are all skills that will benefit the student going forward.

Be that as it may, not all HIPs are created equal. Overnight studies on HIPs have flooded the literature and professional conferences, and the active learning vernacular has been adopted and embraced by our colleagues and administrations. Given that Kuh suggests that students take advantage of two HIPs per academic career, there can be an assumption that more is more. Some believe that the more offerings students take advantage of the better, and the more programs universities offer students, then the more desirable the institution is for admissions. As a result, the students can be distracted and overwhelmed by the myriad of experiential learning opportunities available on campus.

In addition to an overabundance of offerings, the actual value of the specific opportunity can also be a concern. Each activity offered may not equate to an engaged learning experience for the student.[7] It is also common for certain HIPs to be required of students, such as first-year courses or shared intellectual experiences. These required offerings can prove insufficient to advisors for identifying and preparing potential scholarship candidates because it is difficult to gauge the student's initiative and individualized interests.

Examining Undergraduate Research, Service Learning, and Study Abroad

The HIPs that students self-select to participate in, however, can be of particular interest to fellowships advisors. At the University of Houston, we have found the most common activities are undergraduate research, service learning, and study abroad (referred to by Kuh as global learning). Certainly, all three of these activities are valuable to students in heightening their critical thinking, local and global citizenship, communication, and professional development in addition to other attributes. As Table 1.1 demonstrates, there are both pros and cons for fellowships advisement associated with these three activities. Nevertheless, certain components distinguish **undergraduate research** from the other HIPs as particularly advantageous to both students and fellowships advisors.

Undergraduate research inherently promotes the advancement of intellectual development, and one line of inquiry organically leads to another. When students commit to conducting research with a professor, they grow in confidence within the research environment and as researchers. Over time, they can assume leadership roles as researchers by exploring more significant projects, sometimes of their own design. It would be logistically challenging and very costly to structure study abroad activities in a way that could incrementally increase students' level of knowledge, engagement, and leadership each time they travel. Service learning programs offer avenues for students to become more involved each year, but more factors are at play—such as the needs of the community partners, the programs the students serve, and the resources available to continue to grow the

Table 1.1. Pros and Cons for HIPs

High-Impact Practice	Pros for Fellowships Advisement	Cons for Fellowships Advisement
Mentored Undergraduate Research	• Supports independent and sustained learning • Adheres to students' schedules • Cultivates relationships with faculty • Offers opportunities to present and publish • Fosters leadership	• Can be difficult to determine student's specific role within project
Service Learning	• Focuses on community • Supports independent and sustained learning • Adheres to students' schedules • Cultivates relationships with faculty • Fosters leadership	• More complex to arrange project with faculty, student, and community partners • Lower GPA requirement • Can be difficult to determine student's specific role within project
Study Abroad	• Promotes global and cultural awareness • Hones language skills • Can be community focused	• Lower GPA requirement • Timing is less flexible

initiative. The question of sustainability can also be problematic for service learning initiatives due to institutional changes in priorities and personnel; whereas, university faculty appointments and projects are less volatile.

Conducting research is also convenient for students' schedules. Working in a lab or assisting a professor in writing a book can essentially take place at any time. Many students utilize their summer and semester breaks to immerse themselves in conducting research. Service is also a year-round endeavor, but it can be dependent on the academic calendar, particularly for students working in K–12 schools. At many institutions, the timing of when a study abroad might take place during a student's academic career can be restrictive.[8]

Service learning and study abroad opportunities tend to have flexible academic requirements, which fortunately encourage more participation in these activities. However, these participants may not meet the minimum GPA requirements for applying to nationally competitive scholarships. Mentored undergraduate research activities, particularly scholarship programs, are quite selective and necessitate the academic rigor required by the most competitive fellowships. Undergraduate research also promotes the attainment of a doctoral degree.[9,10] Students are surrounded by professors, post-docs, and graduate students, so the notion of earning an advanced degree seems more attainable and desirable. This environment also presents opportunities for undergraduates to present and publish.

Finally, mentored undergraduate research is perhaps *the* best way to build a strong working relationship with a professor. The student and professor are working together intensively in problem-solving and critical analysis, which can pave the way for applying to awards that value research, such as the Barry Goldwater Scholarship and the NSF Graduate Research Fellowship. Certainly, faculty-led service learning projects and study abroad programs also cultivate mentored relationships with professors, but these activities can be cost prohibitive for students. Research service learning activities and research study abroad activities are comparable to traditional mentored research opportunities. These programs, however, are typically more complex to develop and may be less prevalent on college campuses.

Purpose of the HERE Program

Recognizing that undergraduate research has been the most fruitful high-impact practice for scholarship recruitment and advisement efforts, the authors sought to create a novel research program—the Houston Early Research Experience (HERE). This article details the development of HERE, a May-term program offered through the honors college at the University of Houston. The honors college is nationally recognized, providing a small community and enriching liberal arts experience to twenty-five hundred high-achieving students, who also enjoy the benefits of attending a major metropolitan research university. Several of the college's programs, including HERE, serve the entire university, allowing well-qualified undergraduates from across campus to take advantage of research and other opportunities. HERE promotes a culture of research, which is consistent with the University of Houston's designation as a public "R1" institution serving over forty-five thousand students, and one of the most diverse student bodies in the country. The program encourages students to pursue an undergraduate research activity early in their academic career. HERE was also created to serve as a pipeline of students applying for nationally competitive scholarships—particularly freshmen and sophomores.

HERE is qualitatively different from any other initiative the University of Houston offers students. It both *identifies* and *prepares* fellowship candidates and is a gateway initiative for other opportunities. The program accomplishes the following:

- Recruits freshman and sophomore students to pursue faculty-mentored research and apply for major awards upon completion of the program
- Integrates theoretical and applied knowledge early in the students' academic year
- Raises big-picture questions that students must collaborate with one another to answer
- Develops foundational research skills
- Builds relationships between students and faculty members

About the HERE Program

Held during a two-week workshop in May, HERE orients freshmen and sophomores from all majors to the fundamentals of conducting research. The initiative is intended to educate students on the complexities surrounding a major metropolitan city, namely the City of Houston. For example, in 2018 students studied public policy, gaining a better understanding of the many facets of sustainability within their community. Student activities include reading and discussing academic articles with faculty seminar leaders; learning how to ask appropriate, specific research questions when approaching a project; conducting faculty-guided research; going on field

Figure 1.1. Expansion of the HERE Program

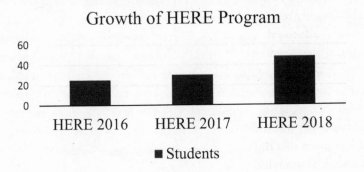

trips; and delivering group presentations on their research topics. Participation in this program is typically the first time students have conducted research at the collegiate level.

Students perceive the HERE program as a valuable experience. As Figure 1.1 demonstrates, during the HERE program's three-year tenure, participation has swelled from twenty-five to forty-eight students annually. Although the program has grown, the faculty-to-student ratios have remained the same, which is pivotal to the success of the initiative. One faculty mentor leads a seminar of approximately six students.

Just like the students, the faculty members represent multiple colleges on campus. The seminar leaders are charged with teaching students how to understand and examine academic articles, guiding the selection of appropriate group research topics, and supporting the development of their projects. Students do not earn course credit for their participation but do receive $1,000 scholarships upon completion of the program. Faculty seminar leaders receive stipends for their involvement. The HERE program receives support from the provost's office, division of research, the engineering college, and the honors college.

Major Award Applicant Identification

Timing of Program. The timing of the HERE program makes it a distinctive high-impact initiative. The two-week program takes place in mid-May—immediately following the close of the spring academic semester but before the summer session begins. This does interfere with some study abroad experiences but has generally proven to be an ideal time to offer an early research experience to students. The campus is quiet. The students are focused. The faculty are available to participate. There are many available meeting spaces and venues at the university. These factors contribute to creating an engaged, reflective mind-set for the students. During the academic semesters, it can be extremely challenging to garner students' full attention. Offering a program between semesters addresses this concern. The students fully immerse themselves in their work. In addition, given that the program takes place at the conclusion of the spring semester, it is more likely to appeal to students who are proactive, motivated, and inspired learners.

Application Process. Applicants must have at least a 3.5 GPA. This is a much higher GPA than that of the university's minimum standards for service learning and study abroad opportunities (Table 1.1). The candidates are assessed by a selection committee who can evaluate for other potential factors that might play a role in applying for a fellowship. For instance, the application is geared toward soliciting information on the candidates' interests outside the classroom and other attributes that would lend themselves to potential interest in major awards. In addition, those who are not accepted into the HERE program can still be considered for other opportunities going forward. Therefore, the application and selection process of HERE in and of itself creates a pool for major award candidates.

Schedule and Assignments. Each day of the program varies slightly. Most often, however, the students start their mornings together to review the day's agenda and receive the group announcements. Next, they meet in their faculty-led small groups to analyze and discuss the journal articles they read in advance of the meeting. Additional professors and community partners are often invited to the small group chats to offer their expertise to the conversations. They then meet as a large group for the guest speaker's presentation. After a lunch break, HERE participants rejoin their small groups to continue their discussion on research and scholarship. The students conclude their day by collaborating on their group research topics and planning for their final presentation. Their faculty seminar leaders are available during this independent research time to offer guidance and direction. The HERE schedule is flexible enough to accommodate for field trips and the final group presentations at the end of the program. The

Figure I.2. HERE Assessment Model

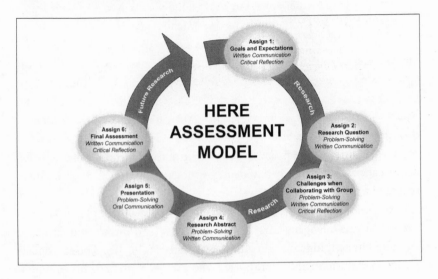

sessions take place in meeting rooms in the honors college and the university library. On-campus residential accommodations are not provided for this program; most students commute to campus each day or arrange for on-campus housing independently.

The students complete a total of six assignments during the two-week program. They submit three critical response essays, the research question, and the research abstract for their projects. The final assignment is a group oral presentation on their selected topic. Reviewing the submissions is an additional way for advisors to learn how effective students are in problem-solving, written communication, and critical reflection, as showcased in Figure 1.2.

The assignments are also a way for students to demonstrate whether they are self-starters and likely to take initiative on projects. The response essays offer multiple opportunities for students to consider their experiences in real time and hone their ability to reflect—an essential ability for scholarship candidates.[11] The assessments are also a means for scholarship advisors to gauge students' interest in major awards and identify students who might be competitive candidates. The final written assignment for HERE addresses major awards directly:

What did you learn both academically and professionally through the HERE experience? As a result of this opportunity, are you more likely to pursue another experiential learning opportunity? If so, which of the following are you considering: SURF, PURS, or a senior honors thesis; an external research opportunity; and/or a nationally competitive scholarship, such as the Critical Language, Fulbright, or Goldwater Scholarships?

Major Award Applicant Preparation

Identify as scholars and leaders. As a result of this experience, the students begin to identify themselves as scholars often for the first time in their academic careers. They realize they can contribute to their fields and are more prepared to take ownership of their learning. By way of example, when the students deliver their oral presentations on the final day of the program, they encounter a lengthy Q&A from faculty and peers. The questions can be quite challenging, further providing an opportunity for a more real-world presentation experience and allowing the students to educate their classmates on a particular topic. The top-scored oral presenters receive a coveted invitation to present their projects at the honors college's lecture series, entitled the Grand Challenges Forum, at the start of the academic year. This lecture series is attended by hundreds of students, faculty, and staff throughout the campus community. Not only does this serve as an incentive to develop a high-caliber presentation, but it also creates a culture of healthy competition among the students. By presenting at the lecture series, they are recognized as leaders among their peers.

Exposure to real world problems. The program exposes students to topical issues, and as a result of the experience, they are more aware of how their discipline is situated within a larger academic context. This can motivate them to become proactive change agents on a societal issue or problem. Similar to the purpose of service learning initiatives, the HERE program is thus able to cultivate civic-minded students. It also plants the seed for the potential to make a difference through research, scholarship, and other activities outside the required curriculum. These efforts tend to be directed with a particular goal in mind, rather than more for the sake of doing more.

The research topic chosen each year is intended to stir intellectual curiosity and debate while also better orienting students to their community. The topic is selected collaboratively by the coordinators and the faculty associated with the program. Criteria for selecting a research topic include issues of saliency, urgency, and relevance for the city of Houston. This enables students from all majors to more fully understand how their academic and personal backgrounds can contribute to the intellectual conversation. In 2016 and 2017, the topic was studying grand challenges within the city of Houston. For 2018, the theme was sustainability and sequestration in Houston. Next year's program will be even more focused: an exploration of flooding in Houston.

Exposure to research. The HERE students conduct research on issues pertaining to both their academic field and community. These projects can provide a foundation for more significant research activities later in their academic careers, paving the way for a successful research record. For instance, upon learning about a faculty member's research in emergency management during a HERE lecture, one student contacted this professor about conducting a faculty-mentored research experience. The project, which eventually became the student's senior honors thesis, evolved into conducting a case study analyzing innovation in health care among medical staff at a local hospital. Throughout the program, the HERE coordinators and the faculty seminar leaders also discuss how to become involved in faculty-mentored research opportunities with the students.

Broadens their academic network. The early student researchers develop relationships with faculty members from a broad range of fields. These faculty members can become the students' research mentors throughout their academic career and can serve as writers for recommendation letters. Over the course of the two-week period, they also form close-knit relationships with peers who are interested in research and scholarship. They will often stay after-hours to collaborate on a research topic or practice their presentations. Since their research presentations stir a lively debate, these types of academic deliberations pave the way for future intellectual discussions and additional avenues for inquiry and analysis. These interactions hone their verbal communication skills in preparation for presenting at future conferences within their field.

Additional Benefits to Fellowships Advisors

Build stronger professional networks. The HERE coordinators form strong working relationships with faculty and community partners affiliated with the program. The program hosts a guest speaker each day, so the visitor may be a faculty member on campus or a member of the greater Houston community. Guest professors comprise a wide range of colleges on campus. External speakers have spanned from representatives from the Environmental Protection Agency and mayor's office to a news anchor, meteorologist, and graffiti artist. These are faculty members and community partners who can be contacted to serve on practice interviews and recruitment efforts going forward. For instance, a faculty member in economics led a seminar on how sequestration would impact Houston. This same professor can now readily be called upon to serve on a practice Fulbright or Truman interview should the candidate's topic be relevant. The HERE faculty participants essentially become allies and ambassadors for the program and can assist in publicizing major awards to their classes and within their departments, referring potential candidates for nationally competitive scholarships.

Encourage participation in experiential learning. Clearly this program is intended to raise awareness for major awards and is a way to proactively advise students, encouraging them to consider and plan their next steps after the program. Upon completion of the HERE program, the students are encouraged to apply to additional programs offered through the Office of Undergraduate Research as well as other experiential learning opportunities (Figure 1.3). The lightly-shaded spheres in the figure depict additional high-impact practices that HERE may encourage; the darker spheres indicate the types of awards students might apply for as a result of participating in the experiential learning activities.

Results (So Far . . .)

Although this program is still early in its development, and thus continues to evolve and improve, 40 percent of the first cohort in 2016 have either applied or plans to apply for a major award. Many of these 2016 HERE alumni are in their junior year, so this percentage may increase over time. There is a propensity for the HERE students to apply for certain types of awards that have an international or research focus, such as the DAAD awards, the Critical Language Scholarship, and research experiences for undergraduates (REUs) at other institutions. These are awards they can readily apply for as underclassmen, which can prepare them to apply for larger opportunities that they will become eligible for later in their careers. Anecdotally, of the 2017 and 2018 HERE cohorts, many have stated that

Figure 1.3. Opportunities Stemming from HERE

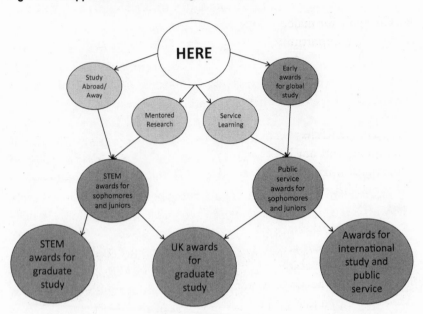

they plan to apply for major awards—mainly the Critical Language, Goldwater, and Fulbright Scholarships. HERE students have also gone on to pursue faculty-mentored research activities and other experiential learning activities.

Although the University of Houston is in the nascent stage of assessing HERE, simply having this program has proven effective. The HERE program is a tangible example of how the honors college is working to create a stronger culture for major awards at the University of Houston. For instance, reports on the HERE program are shared with college and university leadership. HERE was also selected as a showcase program for the university's new Southern Association of Colleges and Schools Commission on Colleges' Quality Enhancement Program (QEP) for 2018. The theme for the university's enhancement program is cocurricular learning, and the QEP leadership team chose HERE to serve as an example of how to administer and assess a successful experiential learning initiative for the campus. The HERE students are also an additional pool of students to call on to serve as ambassadors and representatives for the college and university. They can be asked to serve on university committees or meet with visitors to campus. Most importantly, whether HERE students ultimately apply for major awards or not, they are exposed to a substantive engagement opportunity that enhances their collegiate and professional careers.

Adapting the Model at Other Institutions

Although HERE has been a good fit for the University of Houston, many institutions will not have the bandwidth to launch a new cocurricular program. Asking an administrator or faculty member to develop a novel HIP in addition to the management of major awards—and often other roles such as teaching and administrating—is both daunting and, in some cases, implausible. Nevertheless, recognizing that all HIPs are not created equal, exposing students to research and cohort-building opportunities early in their academic career has value. Some components of this program could be scaled or adapted to fit existing initiatives on other campuses. Given that HERE is only two weeks in length, a version could serve as additional programming within an existing larger effort. This program could also be modified as a smaller scale, invitation-only program with fewer participants, which would be easier to coordinate. This might include nominations from faculty to participate, and perhaps the theme could be tailored once the students were selected. If funding is the limitation, implementation might include providing course credit or even volunteering for the program provided there is an incentive associated with participation.

Going Forward

The most significant challenge has been recruiting students from the arts, humanities, and social sciences into the program. STEM students comprise 70 percent of the total cohort. In efforts to improve representation within fields outside of STEM, recruitment strategies for the program started earlier within the academic year. The information on the 2019 program was live on the website immediately following the 2018 program. More focused recruitment efforts included meeting with advisors and directors of undergraduate study in the arts, humanities, and social sciences in efforts to develop ways to strategically reach their students. The HERE program coordinators have gradually become ambassadors at university recruitment and orientation events, consistently talking to potential students and their parents about HERE.

In addition, the overarching research topic for the program continues to be refined. Although the topic must be broad enough so that students from all fields can benefit and contribute, at the same time, it must be narrow in scope for students to consider ideas and projects they can pursue. For 2019, the HERE topic is much more specific to Houstonians (flooding), but there is a risk of this topic alienating certain fields. To address this concern, artists and writers who explore natural disasters and how they impact individuals in the community will be invited to present to the students. Engineers and scientists who study flooding will also be asked to participate.

Incorporating HIPs into the Fellowships Advisement Process

Although HIPs may vary in regard to their impact and effectiveness, overall experiential learning activities should be embraced when feasible and appropriate. These practices might be incorporated into the work of fellowships advisors in a number of ways. Advisors can develop methods for scholarship candidates to work collaboratively on their applications. More seasoned scholarship applicants can mentor students who are new to the process of applying for awards. A fellowships course can be offered as a means of fostering a shared intellectual experience among applicants. Candidates can also create e-portfolios, digital narratives, or blogs sharing their insights learned through the award application process. As the landscape of higher education continually faces changes and disruptions, staying abreast of emerging trends and illuminating studies is critical and can influence advising practices and serve students more successfully.[12]

Notes

1. George D. Kuh, "Foreword: And Now There Are 11," in *High Impact ePortfolio Practice: A Catalyst for Student, Faculty, and Institutional Learning*, eds. Bret Eynon and Laura M. Gambino (Sterling, VA: Stylus, 2017), vii–xi.

2. George D. Kuh, *High-Impact Educational Practices: What They Are, Who Has Access to Them, and Why They Matter* (Washington, DC: Association of American Colleges and Universities, 2008).

3. Ashley Finley and Tia Brown McNair, *Assessing Underserved Students' Engagement in High-Impact Practices* (Washington, DC: Association of American Colleges and Universities, November 2013), 139.

4. Valerie Chepp, "Equity-Minded High-Impact Learning: A Short-Term Approach to Student-Faculty Collaborative Research," *Humboldt Journal of Social Relations* 39 (2017): 163–75.

5. Kuh, *High-Impact Educational Practices*.

6. National Survey of Student Engagement (NSSE), *Experiences That Matter: Enhancing Student Learning and Success. Annual Report 2007* (Bloomington, IN: Center for Postsecondary Research, 2007), 12.

7. Walter Karna, "Student Engagement: A Road to Travel More," in *Roads Less Traveled and Other Perspectives on Nationally Competitive Scholarships,* eds. Suzanne McCray and Joanne Brzinski (Fayetteville: University of Arkansas Press, 2017), 53–64.

8. Richard Montauk, "Advising Students on the Many Roads of Study Abroad," in *Roads Less Traveled and Other Perspectives on Nationally Competitive Scholarships,* eds. Suzanne McCray and Joanne Brzinski (Fayetteville: University of Arkansas Press, 2017), 75–89.

9. Russel S. Hathaway, Biren A. Nagda, and Sandra R. Gregerman, "The Relationship of Undergraduate Research Participation to Graduate and Professional Education Pursuit: An Empirical Study," *Journal of College Student Development* 43, no. 5 (2002): 614–31.

10. John F. Kremer and Robert G. Bringle, "The Effects of an Intensive Research Experience on the Careers of Talented Undergraduates," *Journal of Research & Development in Education* 24, no. 1 (1990): 1–5.

11. Karna, "Student Engagement."

12. We would like to thank our colleague Mallory Chesser for editing this manuscript. We are grateful for her efforts.

2

Leading by Consensus with Civility and Integrity
The Udall Factor

SUZANNE McCRAY, JANE MORRIS, AND PAULA RANDLER

Suzanne McCray is vice provost for enrollment management, director of the Office of Nationally Competitive Awards, and associate professor in the Higher Education program in the College of Education and Health Professions at the University of Arkansas. She is currently serving as chair of College Board's Southwestern Regional Council. She is also a member of its national Advanced Placement Higher Education Advisory Council and the Capstone Champions Task Force. For three years, she served on the national program review for the Coca-Cola Scholarship, and she is in her twelfth year on the national selection committee for the Morris K. and Stewart L. Udall Scholarship and her third on the Critical Language Scholarship. McCray is an active member of the National Association of Fellowships Advisors, serving as its president from 2003 to 2005. She has edited six volumes of essays on the topic of nationally competitive scholarships. The most recent prior to this volume is Roads Less Traveled and Other Perspectives on Nationally Competitive Scholarships

(2017). She earned a BA (high honors), an MA in English from the University of Arkansas, and a PhD in English from the University of Tennessee.

Jane Morris *is executive director of the Center for Undergraduate Research and Fellowships at the University of Pennsylvania. As executive director, Morris provides leadership and direction for the office at Penn that supports students seeking research experience and opportunities through nationally competitive scholarships. Prior to Penn, Morris served as executive director of Duke's Office of Undergraduate Scholars and Fellows and as director of Villanova's Center for Undergraduate Research and Fellowships. Morris holds a BS in biology from Villanova University, an MA in biology from Bryn Mawr College, and she spent twenty years as a research scientist before moving into higher education. In her leadership roles at Duke and Villanova, Morris not only directed efforts to broaden participation in nationally competitive scholarships, but she also managed undergraduate research efforts at Villanova and internal merit scholarship programs at both Duke and Villanova. Morris is former president of the National Association of Fellowships Advisors, serving as a direct liaison between the scholarship advisors and the leadership of foundations including the Rhodes, the Marshall, the Mitchell, and the Udall. In this role, Morris participated directly in helping the Marshall Scholarship Program evaluate and revise their selection criteria to include those same qualities of intellectual leadership that define excellence in a broader and more meaningful context. Morris believes deeply in the power of engaging students in an authentic process of discernment, articulation, action, and reflection that moves them from the classroom into postgraduate lives where they can make meaningful contributions to the world.*

Paula Randler *is a former program manager at the Udall Foundation and a 2003 alumna of the Udall Scholarship. She has served on the national selection committee for the Morris K. and Stewart L. Udall Scholarship* *three times (both before and after her tenure as program manager), and spent hundreds of hours articulating the Udall Foundation mission and Udall Scholarship leadership objectives to students and faculty alike. During her tenure at the foundation, Randler worked successfully to increase the quality and quantity of Native American and Alaska Native applicants to the scholarship, and explored how the scholarship can benefit additional communities in Indian Country. She is now a program manager at a federal land management agency and a certified career coach, specializing in career transitions and change management. She holds a BS in geological sciences from the University of South Carolina and an MA in environmental management from Yale University's School of Forestry and Environmental Studies. Like many Udall Scholar alumni, she continues to be an active member of the alumni community.*

Scholarship and fellowships advisors spend a great deal of time helping students explore the concept of leadership within the context of the scholarship for which they are applying. While general principles of leadership weave throughout the criteria for many of the major scholarship programs, the Udall Scholarship frames leadership through the lens of civility, integrity, and consensus.[1] Each April, when Udall Scholarship application reviewers gather in Tucson to select the new cohort of Udall Scholars, they participate in an intensive training program that stresses the importance of considering these ideals in assessing applications for leadership, public service, and commitment to issues of the environment or Native American tribal policy or health care. Leadership, when evaluated on this basis, reflects a model of public service, practiced by the Udall family, that strives to effect change by finding common ground through civil discourse.[2]

Established to honor the legacy of Morris K. Udall and Stewart L. Udall, the Udall Foundation holds the values of civility, integrity, and consensus as the foundation for all of its programs. Morris K. Udall represented the State of Arizona in Congress from 1961 to 1991. He served with distinction as a champion for conservation, protection of the environment, and Native American rights. As a liberal serving within a conservative district, Udall used his intelligence, wit, and grace to develop bipartisan alliances that ensured the passage of controversial legislation on environmental protection and political reform. During his first decade in office, he sponsored twelve bills, eleven of which were passed into law. When he retired after thirty years in office, he was so well liked and respected in both houses, by Republicans and Democrats alike, that only five weeks passed before a bipartisan bill was introduced in the Senate to create a foundation in his honor. Throughout this process, colleagues praised his integrity, ability to lead by consensus, legislative achievements, and sense of humor.

The addition of Stewart Udall's name to the Morris K. Udall and Stewart L. Udall Foundation came into existence by an act of Congress in 2009, in recognition of Stewart's historic and visionary environmental contributions. After representing Arizona in Congress for three terms, Stewart Udall served as the Secretary of the Interior from 1961 to 1969 under Presidents Kennedy and Johnson. With a focus on bipartisanship and consensus-building, Udall accomplished the establishment of national parks, wildlife refuges, sea- and lakeshores, and national monuments. Guided by the principles of civility and integrity, the Udall brothers were able to bring both Republicans and Democrats together to address complex issues such as environmental protection, water conservation, and animal protection. This is the concept of leadership that the Udall Foundation seeks in its scholars and that reviewers of scholarship applications are called to evaluate.[3]

Knowing the foundation's mission is critical to a reviewer's understanding about what to look for in applications and how to interpret leadership, service, and chosen career paths. As most advisors know, the Udall Scholarship is awarded in three categories. One is to promote an understanding of and an active engagement with issues connected to the environment (including public policy and conflict resolution), to the use of public lands, and to resource management. Scholars who are selected because of the commitment to pursuing careers in the environment embrace a wide range of interests from green architectural designs to environmentally sensitive finance to environmental impact on wildlife and much more.

Two other categories of the Udall Scholarship support those students whose careers will make a positive impact in Indian Country. Native

American Health Care describes those students who intend careers as doctors, nurses, counselors, social workers, researchers, and public health officials. Their work will have a positive impact on the health of Native people both on and off the reservation. Tribal Public Policy describes a very inclusive category that supports students whose careers will address the sovereignty of Native nations: sustainable governance and financial management; education; cultural preservation including language and art; social services and policies that protect children and women; legal reform, law enforcement, and accountability; economic development; housing and many more.

What Makes a Udall Scholar?

Regardless of the category, reviewers use a rating form[4] as a guide for evaluating applications and assessing those who are selected. The form is a guide that different readers use in slightly different ways with remarkably similar results. Both the form and the instructions on essential characteristics are used as a means to help readers suss out the "Essential Characteristics of a Scholar" that must be met if students are to be selected. These are provided to readers in "A Step by Step Guide to the Udall Application" and include the following:

- **"Commitment**—A deep passion for the environment, tribal policy, or Native health care is evident from the stated career goals, and through activities, service, academic pursuits, references, etc. Involvement in relevant campus or community activities is consistent and ongoing. The application gives insight into the student's motivation or the driving force behind her/his passion.
- **Character** (the Udall factor)—leadership, service, and integrity. Application reveals a desire to make a difference and solve problems. Demonstrated leadership experience goes beyond sitting on a committee or planning an event to motivating others and producing results that benefit the campus or community. References attest to character and potential.
- **Trajectory**—The career goals, activities, and service demonstrate that the student has begun to work towards a career that will allow him/her to make significant contributions to environmental issues,

her/his tribe, or Indian Country in general through political or public service or community action. The reader understands which issues related to the environment, tribal policy, or Native health care the student wants to work on, how they plan to do it, and is convinced that they will go on to use their degree to help Indian people or impact the environment."[5] (Students are, of course, not locked into this plan, but it is important that they understand how to formulate such a plan.)

More about Commitment and Character

In trying to assess a student's commitment to a career in a Udall focus area, readers are looking for students who have ambitious, yet feasible, goals and plans and who show sustained commitment to these issues. Summer jobs, internships, co-op programs, and student-driven campus initiatives can also point to a student who is engaged and will continue that engagement into a career. Even students with heavy family responsibilities or those who work long hours must show some level of activity in these areas. In determining commitment to a Udall focus area, reviewers look for the following:

- Clearly articulated commitment to focus area, supported by relevant coursework and research, postgraduation plans, extracurricular activities, personal investment, and long-term goals
- Goals that span disciplines and aim to solve problems or build consensus
- History of involvement with areas of interest
- Commitment that extends to community and is recognized in letters of recommendation
- For those in tribal policy or health care, career goals that involve working with a tribe or that otherwise benefit Indian Country
- For those in environment category, sustained, consistent environmental commitments, both on campus and in the community
- Jobs and internships in the area of interest
- Letters that acknowledge and reinforce these interests and traits

While the types of supportive evidence listed above help Udall readers to discern the depth of commitment documented in an application, what is not in the application is equally relevant. If reviewers observe the following lack of evidence, the application is unlikely to advance in the review process:

- Goals unsupported by the application (as seen in the activities, jobs, internships, research, coursework, letters of recommendation, and essay)
- Unclear commitment to issues related to the environment, tribal public policy, or health care (nominees show more commitment to other areas like research in general, food insecurity, architecture, etc.)
- Limited, naive, or unrealistic career goals
- No explanation for the focus in one area
- For those in tribal policy or tribal health care, little or no relationship with Native community or uninformed or ill-informed understanding regarding tribal or Indian Country issues
- No leadership in focus area

In assessing the quality of "character," reviewers are not making a personal judgment about the applicant. Rather, they are seeking evidence in the application of the nominee's ability to identify specific problems within the focus area, develop meaningful strategies for addressing those problems, and establish collaborations among a variety of stakeholders to achieve those solutions. In fact, what reviewers seek to identify are those qualities of civility, integrity, and consensus that comprise the "Udall factor." Such evidence can include:

- Solid record of service on the campus or in the community
- Active problem-solving
- Ability to combine theory and application, research and practice
- Nominees who work more than twenty hours a week and who still demonstrate commitment to the field outside coursework
- Good balance among academics, extracurricular activities, or research
- Personal choices that demonstrate commitment

- Being well-rounded (being involved in activities outside the focus area—sports, art, drama, etc.)
- References that attest to character and intellect

Less helpful in assessing the "Udall factor" are the following:

- Few or only very recent activities (campus, community, research, jobs, or internships) outside coursework related to the nominee's interest in the environment, tribal public policy, or Native American health care
- No demonstrated leadership
- No service of any kind
- Nominees who point out problems but no solutions
- Nominees who wax lyrical about their plans to engage with the environment, public, or Native American health care but have not sustained any in-depth work in the area
- Unhelpful letters that simply list activities, GPA, or performance on coursework
- A lack of response to the additional information section or a thank-you or request for funding in this section

Leadership, the Udall Way

In *Leading the Way: Student Engagement and Nationally Competitive Awards*, Tara Yglesias wrote a compelling essay about the importance of clearly demonstrating leadership in a Truman application.[6] She observed that leadership is an important part of the criteria for many scholarships, but that the way it is assessed is unique to each program. Like many scholarships, the Udall considers leadership an important element to any successful application, but alone it is not sufficient for selection. In the selection of Udall Scholars, leadership must exist in the context of both commitment and character. Leadership highlighted by the Udall core values of "civility, integrity, and consensus" can resonate in many parts of the Udall application. Advisors who read the article designed for Truman applicants and apply it wholesale to Udall candidates on their campuses may be doing a disservice to their students. Of course, Truman applicants must embody civility and integrity, but where a leadership essay in a Truman application may focus more on what the student applying accomplished (the "I" essay), the Udall leadership essay may need to focus at some point on building the team and bringing about consensus (an "I" leading to a "we" essay).

The Udall application, like the Truman and Marshall Scholarship applications, contains a specific question about the applicant's leadership experience and how they have made a difference on their campuses or in their communities (Question 5). For many Udall readers, this question and the question about the student's most significant public service activity (Question 7) are central to understanding the student's level of commitment. Evaluating a Udall leadership response for a specific example of leading through consensus, Udall reviewers assess how applicants articulate not only their individual roles, but also how they motivated others to form successful collaborations. There is no cookie-cutter answer that invariably works, but some aspect of team building should be evident and should also include:

- A vision of what is important and how it can be accomplished
- Leadership experience that goes beyond a title
- The buy-in of others—student groups, administrators, relevant committees, agencies, and nonprofits
- Details of implementing strategy and dealing with obstacles to accomplishment
- Documented outcomes—even those that were not expected
- Some connection to the student's field of study or academic goals, environmental or Native American concerns (depending on application) or career aspirations

Less helpful for a review of Udall leadership:

- The nominee's title (student government president, committee chair, treasurer, etc.) without active engagement
- Limited outreach to a small or privileged group
- No long-term plan or chance of sustainability
- Nominee leads by doing everything
- No documentable or substantiated (letter of reference) difference being made

An application can be particularly strong if the student's career goal is addressed at several points throughout the application showcasing the many facets of commitment, including in the leadership and public service questions as mentioned here, and also in the list of important activities, additional information, and the "long essay" or "Udall essay."

The Udall Essay and Leadership

The Udall essay is an opportunity for nominees to demonstrate their academic abilities by carefully researching the writings, speeches, and legislative acts of the Udalls. Choosing the one that is a good fit for a student's long-term goals is important. Students who simply latch on to the first speech they find and make it fit may not write a compelling essay. The most popular choices are essays like Morris Udall's speech "Environment vs. Economy: Exploding a Phony Issue" or "The Environment at Valley Forge." For some students, choosing one of these is the right choice, matching well with their own assessments of environment, energy, and/or economic issues and fitting nicely with their career paths. For many it is not, causing students to do some writing gymnastics to force a meaningful connection. Nominees should be able to demonstrate a deep understanding of the piece they choose, placing it in some sort of historical context. Nominees do not always have to agree with or pay homage to the Udalls, but they must engage in some compelling way with the ideas presented.

This essay should also be as much about the student as it is about Morris or Stewart Udall. The prompt tells nominees to choose a significant writing, speech, or legislative act and describe its impact on their own "field of study, interests, and career goals." Writing convincingly about themselves seems to be the most difficult part of the assignment. Too often students provide plot summaries of the Udall piece they have selected, adding a paragraph at the end that points to a personal connection. Such essays are not effective. They fail on both sides of the assignment, offering very little insight to their own scholarly work and objectives, and exhibiting little understanding of Morris or Stewart Udall's political aims.

The Udall essay is not intended to be a personal statement or resume in narrative form, nor is it intended to be a *Cliff Notes* entry on a Udall work. Readers look for essays that do a good job of integrating the nominee's career interests with an understanding of Udall through an appropriately selected work. Many reviewers reread the student's career goals immediately prior to reading this essay to make sure the connections between the student's goals and the Udall piece chosen are clearly made. A fresh take is always fun for the reader, but it is not required of all those selected as scholars. A competent look at a Udall work, combined effectively with a compelling connection to the student's career path, is required.

What It Means to Be a Udall Scholar

The Udall Scholarship selection is an intense process, conducted over the course of four days, that ensures that each application is read by multiple reviewers and assessed for its representation of the Udall Foundation mission to "provide programs to promote leadership, education, collaboration, and conflict resolution in the areas of environment, public lands, and natural resources in order to strengthen Native nations, assist federal agencies and others to resolve environmental conflicts, and to encourage the continued use and appreciation of our nation's rich resources."[7]

The review committee consists of multiple stakeholders, from academics to experts in the Udall focus areas to Udall Scholars alumni, many of whom remain connected to the Udall Foundation through sanctioned programming or informal engagement with their Udall peers. The applications are reviewed by reading pairs, which often include an academic or an experienced fellowships advisor and a Udall Scholar alum for environmental applications, and Native American health or public policy practitioners and Udall Scholars alumni for applications connected to Native American public health care or tribal policy. These pairs chose one hundred finalists who have the qualifications and the potential to be Udall Scholars. Those one hundred applications are then reread by a different reviewer pair. At the conclusion of this thorough and thoughtful process, the reviewers select fifty new scholars and fifty who earn an honorable mention. Noting the challenge of making these choices from among the many worthy applicants, reviewers observe that Udall applicants as a whole are an amazingly passionate group. Many are leaders in the Udall mold. This selection task is made easier by the guidance provided by the foundation. The end result has been a consistently excellent scholar class and a growing base of alumni who, regardless of the year they were selected or their particular interest area, have gone on to exceptional work in their fields.

When new Udall Scholars gather in Tucson during the annual Udall Scholarship orientation, they quickly learn that they are part of a network of similarly committed change agents for protection of the environment and for promoting Native American tribal policy or health care. They participate in programming that consists of training in the Udall leadership style and work together to solve complex environmental resource case studies designed to introduce them to the power of engaging multiple stakeholders around such issues. They learn negotiating skills, presentation skills, and the importance of including various perspectives to achieve goals.

What may surprise new scholars is the personal investment of the Udall family in the programs that honor their family legacy. Each year, members of the current Udall family of public servants join the orientation programming to personally connect with the scholars and demonstrate their commitment to the ideals of Morris K. and Stewart L. Udall. In essence, each new Udall Scholar becomes part of the Udall family and legacy.

In a world where climate change is proceeding at an unexpectedly rapid pace, where catastrophic weather events result in mass destruction and loss of life, and where habitat loss threatens species extinction, the leadership of Udall Scholars has never been more important. In a country where Native Americans comprise the majority of Americans living in extreme poverty, where Native Americans die at higher rates than other Americans, and where the educational achievement gap for Native American students is wider than for any other minority group, the leadership of Udall Scholars has never been more important. In a country whose leadership is fragmented and stifled by ideology and partisanship, the leadership of Udall Scholars offers an alternative approach. More than sixty years ago, Morris K. and Stewart L. Udall established a vision and achieved critical progress on these issues that we face today through leadership that built consensus through civility and integrity. The work of the Udall family continues in the scholars selected in their honor. It also continues in all of the students who engage in the process of applying for the scholarship and in the work of scholarship advisors who encourage them to apply and who guide them through the process.

Notes

1. As any advisor or student who has been on the Udall web page knows, the words civility, integrity, and consensus appear directly under the foundation logo.

2. The opinions expressed in this article represent those of experienced fellowships advisors and Udall Scholarship reviewers, but not necessarily those of the Udall Foundation.

3. See Udall.gov for additional information on the Udalls and the Udall Foundation.

4. See https://www.udall.gov/Documents/pdf/RatingForm.pdf.

5. Ibid.

5. Udall Foundation Reader Materials, "A Step by Step Guide to the Udall Application," last sent to reviewers on March 5, 2019.

6. Tara Yglesias, "Non Ducor, Duco: Leadership and the Truman Scholarship Application," in *Leading the Way: Student Engagement and Nationally Competitive Awards*, ed. Suzanne McCray (Fayetteville: University of Arkansas Press, 2009).

7. See the Udall Foundation mission statement in the *Udall Foundation Strategic Plan 2018–2022*, https://udall.gov/documents/aboutus /UdallFoundation2018-2022StrategicPlanFINALDecember142017.pdf.

3

Excellent Sheep or Passionate Weirdos? Fellowships and Fellowships Advising as Vehicles for Self-Authorship

RICHELLE BERNAZZOLI, JOANNA DICKERT, ANNE MOORE, AND JASON KELLY ROBERTS

Richelle Bernazzoli is assistant director of Undergraduate Research and National Fellowships at Carnegie Mellon University. She holds a PhD in political geography from the University of Illinois and received a 2011–2012 Fulbright grant to Croatia in order to conduct her dissertation research on the Euro-Atlantic integration process. Bernazzoli taught and advised undergraduates in the Department of Geography before transitioning to fellowships advising with the National and International Scholarships Program at the University of Illinois. She joined the Undergraduate Research Office and Fellowships and Scholarships Office at Carnegie Mellon in 2016, where she has developed a workshop series on research design and proposal development, served as the Fulbright Program Advisor and campus representative for several other awards, and taught in the Department of History. Prior to entering academia, Bernazzoli served in the Army National Guard and completed a peacekeeping deployment in Kosovo.

Joanna Dickert *is interim director of the Office of Community Standards and Integrity (OCSI) at Carnegie Mellon University. Currently in her fifteenth year at Carnegie Mellon, her previous work has included program development and student engagement related to undergraduate research, national fellowships advising, academic integrity, and women's leadership. In addition to her work in OCSI, Dickert is a PhD student in the Department of Evaluation and Measurement at Kent State University. Through the alignment of a student-centered process with an evidence-based approach to decision making, she is interested in exploring how assessment and evaluation can improve student learning, particularly in meta-curricular experiences. Dickert has taught introductory business management and leadership courses at Duquesne University, as well as courses on social responsibility at Carnegie Mellon. She currently serves as a member of the Advanced Placement (AP) Research Development E-portfolio.*

Anne Moore *is program specialist in scholar development at Tufts University. She holds a PhD in English literature from Tufts University, where she previously worked at the Academic Resource Center as a graduate writing consultant and the diversity outreach coordinator for the writing program. While completing her graduate work at Tufts, she taught in the English Department and the Women and Gender Studies Department. Her dissertation,* After the Break: Excess, Affect, and the Serial Form, *is under contract with McFarland Press. She has worked in the Office of Scholar Development since 2012. In that position, she serves as point person for all nationally competitive fellowships and scholarships and administers Tufts's summer undergraduate research program. Prior to entering academia, Moore taught special education on the high school level in Burlington, Vermont, and was a founding board member of the Pride Center of Vermont.*

Jason Kelly Roberts *is assistant director in Northwestern University's Office of Fellowships, where he works primarily with first- and second-year students and with applicants for awards in the United States. In summer 2016, he co-organized the first Midwest Fellowships Advising Symposium, which considered the topic of inclusive advising practices. He received his PhD in screen cultures from Northwestern and wrote his dissertation on the history of film criticism across several moments of major technological change; a portion of this research, entitled "So Meaninglessly Present: Pauline Kael Watches Movies on TV," appears in* Talking about Pauline Kael: Critics, Filmmakers, and Scholars Remember an Icon. *He is also associate chair in the Humanities Residential College at Chapin Hall, where he is founder and host of the Chapin Cinema Club. In 2017, he received the T. William Heyck Award for his contributions to Chapin.*

Fellowships Advising and the Promise and Problems of Higher Education

This essay seeks to initiate a discussion that contextualizes the work of fellowships advising more squarely within the core mission of higher education—and with that, debates over what ails higher education. Fellowships advisors identify as educators. Many teach (if not in the classroom, in workshop settings), evaluate student work, and increasingly assess the fellowships advising enterprise in terms of learning outcomes and gains in aptitude. Such work has vast potential to help students more thoughtfully navigate their education and their lives. At the same time, this corner of academia bears a responsibility to critically reflect on how our work with fellowships can reproduce structures of privilege rather than challenge them. Perhaps more fundamentally, prestigious awards and the work advisors do to promote them, recruit for them, and help students earn them do not serve a meaningful and productive purpose if recipients approach the awards as the next hoop to jump through on a path toward an externally defined version of success.

William Deresiewicz's 2014 book *Excellent Sheep: The Miseducation of the American Elite and the Way to a Meaningful Life*[1] contributes to the ongoing debate over the purpose of higher education and whether it lives up to its promise of enhancing life at multiple scales—individual, societal, and global. Deresiewicz's is but one voice in a growing body of work that ranges from systematic, longitudinal studies, such as Arum and Roksa's 2010 book *Academically Adrift*,[2] to evidence-driven commentary, such as Zimmerman's July 2018 piece in *The Chronicle of Higher Education*, "Our Best and Brightest Bankers."[3] The debate can be distilled down to two competing views of college. On the one hand is the conception of college that is prevalent outside of academia: higher education as a credentialing experience leading to better jobs, higher pay, and enhanced social status. The alternative conception is that of college as part of a larger project of intellectual discovery and development.

For Deresiewicz, these views represent, respectively, what college *is* (or has become) and what college *should be*. The culture of higher education, in his view, has shifted over time to one that valorizes affluence, credentials, and prestige over meaningful learning. The support services that augment student life have adjusted accordingly. Career centers, for example, are typically oriented around what is often referred to as the "big four": law, medicine, finance, and consulting. As students and families invest heavily in their college experiences, as well as their pathways leading up to college, students are increasingly risk-averse, stunting their capacity for intellectual exploration. Alongside these trends, education has become overspecialized and technocratic, producing workers (not to mention managers) who are hyperindividualistic and given to working within existing structures of power rather than challenging them.[4]

Likewise, student engagement outside of the classroom suffers from similar pressures. Just as they had to in order to gain entrance to college (particularly highly selective institutions), U.S. students in college are expected to excel in cocurricular activities while maintaining sterling academic records to ensure that they gain entrance into the next highly selective opportunities: law school, medical school, prestigious fellowships, and so on. This culture tends to fetishize "service" and "leadership" experiences that are easily packaged for various kinds of audiences to the disadvantage of more solitary, reflective pursuits that can be crucial to artistic and scientific breakthroughs.[5] Too often, this frenetic existence does not accord students the time or space to reflect on whether their intended pathways are, indeed, the ones that will allow them to lead their lives or impact the world in the way they most desire. This is what is meant by the term "excellent sheep": "Students who are smart, talented, and driven, but also anxious, timid and lost, with little intellectual curiosity and a stunted sense of purpose . . . great at what they're doing, but with no idea why they're doing it."[6] What is lost in this achievement arms race is deep engagement with the intellectual content of a university education. Arum and Roksa found that only one-third of the college students studied had made meaningful gains in critical thinking or complex reasoning[7]—skills that are needed in order to make sense of the world, make discerning judgments about moral and ethical issues, and generally achieve complex learning outcomes.[8]

Deresiewicz is speaking from his particular experience of teaching for many years at Yale and counting Ivy League schools among his own alma maters. Indeed, the subtitle of his book (*The Miseducation of the American Elite* . . .) makes clear that he does not intend to implicate all of American academe in his observations. Deresiewicz's critics have pointed out that even within Ivy League schools, varying levels of privilege are represented in student bodies, and students from less affluent backgrounds may approach their education with a different mindset.[9] Many of these trends, if less pronounced at other types of institutions, have taken hold across the landscape of higher education, as evidenced by the representative literature referenced above. Many who write critically about the purpose and efficacy of higher education today would likely concur with Deresiewicz's proposal that rather than train "leaders," educators should focus on training citizens and thinkers, individuals capable of questioning the powerful rather than "competing to become them."[10]

There are clearly several key points of connection from this literature to the work of fellowships advising. Professional fellowships advisors view their programs as being much more than just clearinghouses for funding opportunities. Fellowships advising can and must play an educational role in students' lives, but can fellowships advisors be part of the fundamental cultural shift that Deresiewicz and others call for in higher education?

Fellowships advisors often work with students who have never experienced anything but success—honors students, campus leaders, research superstars, interns at top companies. But the flip side to such successful track records is that they may have been making the reliably lucrative, externally valid choices along this path. As social mobility has stalled, the global employment marketplace is becoming ever more competitive, making it increasingly difficult for college graduates to differentiate themselves from their high-achieving peers. This reinforces the functional appeal of fellowships, despite foundations' lofty missions of seeking and nurturing the sorts of creative, intellectually adventurous, and value-driven thinkers signified by Deresiewicz's phrase "passionate weirdos." Counteracting students' instincts to take the safest routes academically (so as to ensure flawless grades) is difficult when we are compelled to present the realistic profile of, say, a Churchill Scholar (likely someone who has never earned a "B" grade in college).

The inability to make intentional choices regarding educational and professional trajectories means that many students, conditioned to jump through hoops, find themselves nearing graduation with little more than a plan to jump through yet another hoop to attain the next prestigious opportunity. Too often, this is how sought-after awards such as the Rhodes and Gates Cambridge Scholarships are approached.

This blinkered view of prestigious fellowships has implications for how advisors recruit for and educate students about them. There is a tension at the center of the enterprise: advisors have broad agreement that early engagement should be a goal of the profession—it serves a greater educational purpose than mere identification of ideal scholarship applicants in time for them to apply. The difficulty lies in executing this early engagement without conveying the message, "Here's how you need to spend the next few years if you want to be a Rhodes Scholar."

An important consideration here is the role of instructors and academic advisors. As Deresiewicz and others have pointed out, what many students in the current academic culture crave is quality mentorship from trusted advisors who can help them think in different ways about their choices and push them to cultivate their identities. The fellowships advising role allows us to push back on students' professed interests, ideas, and goals in ways that few other mentors have an opportunity to do. But challenging students in this way requires that they approach fellowship applications with the aim of meaningful introspection and intellectual growth, something that is difficult to inspire in them if it runs counter to the ways in which they have been groomed throughout their education.

Finally, this debate has implications for how we define the growth and success of our offices and report our contributions to external audiences. What are our strategic goals? What is expected of merit awards offices? If the answer is to grow the number of applicants (let alone recipients) from one year to the next, does this inevitably lead to practices of *grooming* students for awards rather than helping students to *self-author* their own journeys, whether or not those journeys lead to prestigious fellowships? These questions are addressed in the next section, which examines the concept of self-authorship as one that can serve as a guidepost in the work we do with students. If fellowships advisors are to leverage their advising roles to foster meaningful learning in students, understanding and engaging with students' processes of meaning making is a key component of our ability to do so.

Supporting Students on the Journey to Self-Authorship

Although not necessarily new, the concept of self-authorship has particular relevance to fellowships advising given this discourse. Present in the higher education literature since 1982, self-authorship was first conceptualized by Robert Kegan, who noted that self-authorship represents a shift from an external to an internal locus of meaning making. From Kegan's perspective, self-authored individuals "can coordinate, integrate, act upon, or invent values, beliefs, convictions, generalizations, ideals, abstractions, interpersonal loyalties, and intrapersonal states. It is no longer authored by them; it authors them and thereby achieves a personal authority."[11] This personal authority frees self-authored individuals of external constraints driven by expectations of others, resulting in decision making that is guided by individual values and aspirations.[12]

One of the best-known researchers in this domain is Marcia Baxter Magolda. With a longitudinal study spanning more than twenty years, Baxter Magolda has followed participants in their journey to self-authorship beginning during their undergraduate tenures and continuing into adulthood. Using a constructivist grounded theory approach, she conducted a series of annual interviews with her participants.[13] Her work began with one hundred traditional-age undergraduate students in 1986, of which seventy remained by their postcollege years. By 2008, thirty participants remained. Through her work, Baxter Magolda identified three primary elements of self-authorship: *trusting the internal voice* that is achieved through conflict and questioning; *building an internal foundation* that entails "synthesizing . . . identities, relationships, beliefs and values into a coherent set of internal commitments from which to operate"; and *securing internal commitments* in which individuals assume ownership of their authentic selves and use the internal foundation as the locus for decision making.[14]

Attainment of self-authorship is a lengthy process. Baxter Magolda identified four stages of development.[15] In the first phase, *Following External Formulas*, individuals emulate Deresiewicz's excellent sheep. They follow the perceived path to success, doing what they are told with little deviation from the preordained path. Eventually, dissatisfaction that sometimes culminates in crisis leads individuals to the second phase, *Crossroads*. In this phase, individuals acknowledge that these external influences do not guarantee personal fulfillment and begin to acknowledge the importance of the aforementioned internal foundation. As individuals progress into the third phase, *Becoming the Author of One's Own Life*, they come to embrace uncertainty and complexity, increasingly making decisions that reflect their authentic selves. Often a tumultuous process, Baxter Magolda notes, "This emerging sense of self [requires] renegotiation of existing relationships that had been built on external approval at the expense of personal needs and the creation of new mutual relationships consistent with the internal voice."[16] By the time individuals reach the fourth and final phase, *Internal Formulas*, they have learned to navigate the tension between the internal and external, drawing from the internal foundation to cultivate lives of meaning and authentic relationships.

Although Baxter Magolda began her inquiry with undergraduate students, she acknowledges that most traditional-age undergraduate students will not navigate a path to self-authorship by the end of their undergraduate careers. Rather, their college and university experiences often lead them to a point of transition, a crossroads. This second stage in the development of self-authorship spans a decade or more in young adulthood. In Baxter Magolda's 2001 study, participants report that tensions stemming from professional decisions driven by external influences, as well as the need for individuals to function independently in their respective professional environments, often lead them to this vantage point.[17] While the undergraduate tenure is an important phase in the journey to self-authorship,

Baxter Magolda's findings substantiate the observations of Deresiewicz and others who encounter students whose choices are shaped largely by external influences.

Though the bulk of the scholarship on self-authorship illuminates an important element of this discourse, these developmental pathways are not universal. For example, Pizzolato suggests that students who have historically been underrepresented in higher education may reach the point of self-authorship by their twenties, or in some cases even before they enter college: "Navigating the college decision process may thus catalyze self-authorship because these students may be forced to develop their own formulas for becoming successful—for becoming college students."[18] Moreover, the examination of ethnic identity[19] and sexual orientation identity[20] within the broader discourse of self-authorship reveals additional layers of complexity at each stage of the developmental pathway.

Given this context, what role can advisors and educators in higher-education environments reasonably expect to play in these journeys to self-authorship? Baxter Magolda and King posit that reflective conversations may provide such an avenue.[21] The potential of reflective conversations as educational moments represents an important insight derived from the Wabash National Study of Liberal Arts Education, a mixed-methods longitudinal study conducted at nineteen institutions of higher education beginning in 2006. Self-authorship and the process by which students develop in this domain via the liberal arts were guiding themes within the qualitative portion of the study.[22,23,24] This phase of the study included individual interviews with student participants at six of the participating institutions. These students completed sixty- to ninety-minute interviews each year over the course of four years. Initial interviews were completed with 315 students. Of the original 315 students, 228 completed the second, and 204 likewise completed the third. The fourth and final interview included 177 students.

The interview protocols were designed to function as reflective conversations that "helped students consciously analyze their assumptions about the world, themselves, and their relationships."[25] The interviews were based on the assumption that reflective conversations occur in four stages:

1. Getting acquainted and building rapport
2. Encouraging reflection about important experiences

3. Encouraging interpretation of these reflections
4. Concluding thoughts

Although developed for the purpose of the study, Baxter Magolda and King noted that the questions could be useful for academic advisors and other educators seeking to promote reflective practice for their students. Academic advisors are well positioned to navigate these discussions not only for purposes of pragmatic decision making but also to cultivate these habits of mind. Indeed, Baxter Magolda and King developed a conversation guide with specific questions to further illuminate the process, noting that "the key element is encouraging students to make sense of their experience rather than the educator making sense of it for them."[26]

In this respect, fellowships advisors are similarly situated within the academic enterprise. Serving as guides for students as they navigate complex application processes, fellowships advisors often help students reflect on key moments of challenge and transformation in their development as scholars and citizens. In fact, the timing of applications for postgraduate fellowships may be particularly well suited for these types of interactions. Baxter Magolda and King note that "encouraging [students] to reflect on their experiences and consider why they found them useful helped students consciously analyze their assumptions about the world, themselves, and their relationships."[27] This reflective practice is a key element in the development of self-authorship and one that is not predicated upon a successful application and subsequent award but rather the process of preparing the application itself.

This model provides an important lens through which to examine the pedagogical mission of the field of fellowships advising and encourage transformational rather than transactional student engagement with the application processes. Rapport building is a key component to this relationship, which sets the stage for subsequent interactions and reflection. However, this requires a degree of buy-in from students who must necessarily set aside presumptions that fellowships advisors possess a knowledge of a formula or script for a successful application, a means to an end rather than an end unto itself.

Similarly, the application process can be constructed in a way that promotes reflection practice through formalized prewriting exercises that could be foundational to the application materials themselves. Although constrained to some extent by parameters of individual competitions and constituent application parameters, it is worthwhile to consider how such exercises could be employed to uncover nuance, depth, and complexity in students' lived experiences. Such practices might not only serve the more practical purposes related to initial draft development and subsequent recursion but also facilitate self-reflection as students further navigate development at the crossroads. The habits of mind that directly support meaningful reflection include the embrace of the lived experience with all of its richness and complexity. In this respect, feminist pedagogy can be instructive for advisors and educators and deserves analysis here.

Feminist Pedagogy: Escape from Prestige Island

Fellowships advisors help students gain access to systems of power and prestige, to move up in the hierarchies that structure our society. But in order to win those fellowships, especially those that prize leadership and a vision for social change, advisors encourage students to plumb a line of reasoning—personal experience and emotional investment—that is often denigrated by the hierarchical system in which they have gained success thus far. For instance, Vanderbilt University's "Guide to Feminist Pedagogy" points out how even Paolo Friere, the unofficial patron saint of radical teaching, "embraced the Western view that rationality is the pathway to knowledge and thus, he believed, the best response to oppression: opinions and actions should be based on reason, not emotion."[28] On the one hand, movement from the personal to the abstract makes sense—a large part of the mission of higher education is to teach students to see the world beyond the limits of their own perspective. But this broader viewpoint often comes at the cost of their ability to make connections between their own experiences and emotions. When it comes time to analyze and unpack their own motivations for a scholarship essay, students from privileged backgrounds may feel like their lives are too boring to merit narration; students from outside those systems of privilege (e.g., queer, poor, black, and brown students) sometimes worry that they may be seen as "pandering," or they distrust their own voices in the first place. Strategies of self-authorship offer a way out of both of these potential dilemmas.

Fellowship applications thus offer a unique opportunity for students to approach their own experience anew, using the broader, more abstract perspective they have gained through their undergraduate training to make sense of the emotions and experiences that make up their daily lives. Feminist pedagogy, with its commitment to taking seriously the knowledge that comes from lived experience, provides an ideal toolbox to address these problems. To be clear, this is not about the content of students' projects or their own political orientation—this is about the power relationships that structure academia, including fellowships advising. Using feminist pedagogy empowers advisors to move away from an ends-oriented understanding of the application process while also helping recruit and retain students from underrepresented backgrounds. Because feminist pedagogy rejects the notion of mastery as the end aim of education, it is a particularly valuable way to help students see models of achievement that focus on self-authorship rather than external approval.

Four central principles of feminist pedagogy that can be useful when advising students on fellowships include transparency, nonhierarchical relationships, positional knowledge, and an orientation around process rather than ends. The following discussion outlines specific ways these principles can be translated into practice and the benefits of doing so.

TRANSPARENCY

One concrete benefit of transparency is that it demystifies the process of achievement for students, helping encourage their own sense of full participation in their academic journey. This is also a great way to ensure that advisors are living up to the National Association of Fellowships Advisors' own core value of fairness. To that end, it is important to devise strategies for transparency. Such strategies can include publishing the rubrics used by campus selection committees; debriefing students who are not selected; and giving students copies of their endorsement letters, excising any quotes from other letters.

In this way, whether students win or not, they will emerge from the application process with concrete ways of understanding their own academic and professional experience. Sharing endorsement letters with students can be particularly valuable for students from underrepresented groups, who often experience imposter syndrome. Having an external narrative of their own strengths offers them language that can help them understand and access those strengths more easily.

NONHIERARCHICAL RELATIONSHIPS

There are two kinds of relationships that the advisor can make more equitable: the one between the advisor and the applicant, and among the applicants themselves. When advisors put these relationships on a more even playing field, students find it easier to focus on the application process rather than seeking to gain approval from the advisor or outperform their peers. Given the competitive nature of fellowships, these techniques can help carve out a space where students experience the application process as an opportunity to honestly assess and narrate their academic experiences more than as a performance for a powerful audience.

In terms of the relationship between the advisor and the applicant, it is disingenuous to say that there is no hierarchical relationship. After all, advisors serve on the committees that determine whether a student can apply for an opportunity. The goal should be to offer as much transparency as possible about the nature of that relationship, thus demystifying the power differential. Specific strategies to this end include student-centered pedagogical techniques, usually lifted from rhetoric and composition (e.g., asking questions, refraining from in-line commentary on essays); clarifying the difference between evaluation and support, and delegating essay support when the advisor is a voting member of a selection committee; using participatory learning techniques such as giving examples from the advisor's own research and writing; and actively participating in cultural and academic events on campus. In this way, students have the opportunity to see the relationship between themselves and the advisor as one part of their larger intellectual community.

In terms of mitigating competition among students, it is paramount to de-prioritize GPA as the primary measure of student success. We can do this by removing any GPA recommendation or requirement when we solicit student names from faculty (this is not always possible as some fellowships and scholarships have very specific requirements that faculty need to know so that they do not set up a student for immediate disappointment), and by also emphasizing service and research programs that do not prioritize academic performance over all other elements. Peer writing workshops also help to create a strong sense of community among applicants. For some institutions, it can be helpful to avoid nominating multiple students from the same region for fellowships where they would be competing with one another. Finally, institutional recognition and celebration of fellowships such as end-of-year celebrations should include all applicants, not just recipients. Along the same lines, inviting students who have applied for but not received fellowships to speak on recruitment panels goes a long way toward demystifying the rewards that come from the application process itself.

POSITIONAL KNOWLEDGE

One of the core tenets of feminist theory is positional knowledge: in the words of Donna Haraway, "Feminist objectivity is about limited location and situated knowledge, not about transcendence and splitting of subject and object. It allows us to become answerable for what we learn how to see."[29] Fellowship applications offer students the opportunity to consider their intellectual and service pursuits in light of the specifics of their own social position, so the feminist concept of positional knowledge is particularly useful. When advisors acknowledge how our own experiences have affected our varied career paths (as applicants for opportunities like the ones they are pursuing, as academics and researchers, as community organizers, etc.), this provides the opportunity to model for students the value of personal experience in relation to broader academic and social impact.

There are a number of concrete ways in the processes of recruitment and advising that we can encourage students to value positional knowledge. Sometimes it can be as simple as checking in at the beginning of an advising session and asking students about their lives outside the context of academics. Along the same lines, framing initial questions about students' interest in fellowship opportunities in the broadest possible terms helps them to consider the entire context of their life as relevant to their fellowship goals. Statements like "what's your story?" can go a long way in this regard. When recruiting students for opportunities, consider conducting outreach and workshops at the places that are central to student life more broadly: culture centers, service organizations, even fraternities and sororities. This context signals to students that all their experiences are relevant to their long-term goals, not just the ones that they are encouraged to categorize as "achievements" like academics or student government.

VALUING PROCESS OVER OUTCOME

All these strategies work together to try to help students value the process of applying over the specific outcome. Many of NAFA's best practices aim toward this goal. For instance, in the "Guidelines for Institutions" section of the NAFA *Code of Ethics*, universities are encouraged to "emphasize, through publicity and infrastructure, the value of students' intellectual and personal development through the fellowship process" and to "use techniques that attempt to measure the value of the process of applying for fellowships" when evaluating applications.[30] As this NAFA statement indicates, most advisors already emphasize process over outcome, at least in how they define application processes, if not in how their programs are evaluated by their institutions. That being said, it is valuable to consistently bring students back to the value of the process as an independent thing from whatever they might gain from the specific opportunity. After all, the only benefit on which they can absolutely rely is the chance to honestly represent their experiences, desires, and beliefs.

Taken together, these practices have worked to help students take greater risks in their application materials and to be more authentic in their writing. Moreover, the emphasis on the rewards of the process of applying helps them let go of the idea that achievement is equal to self-actualization. However, another key facet of self-authorship in fellowships is the fellowship experience itself. While the process of applying is an important vehicle for students to find their voices and represent themselves in honest and convincing ways, the nature of the specific program they may be embarking on is another important consideration. It is helpful for advisors to recognize that the best-known, most prestigious fellowships may not always provide the experiences that would best fit our students' journeys toward their most fulfilled selves. The fourth and final section will explore this idea and offer alternatives for advisors and students to consider.

Self-Authorship in Lesser-Known Fellowships

This section of the essay focuses on the potential of lesser-known fellowships to help students avoid the pitfalls that concern Deresiewicz and move toward self-authorship. Highlighted here are the experiences of two recent college graduates, Karen and Rafa, as they pursued and secured positions at the FAO Schwarz Fellowship and Project Horseshoe Farm Fellowship, respectively. This discussion developed through conversations with Karen and Rafa as well as Priscilla Cohen, executive director of the FAO Schwarz Fellowship, and John Dorsey, director of the Project Horseshoe Farm

Fellowship. Through these conversations it became clear that Karen and Rafa did indeed experience the kind of personal growth associated with self-authorship—and that their growth occurred by design.

Before discussing Karen and Rafa's experiences at greater length, a brief overview of the above awards is warranted. Descendants of Frederick A. O. Schwarz created the FAO Schwarz Family Foundation (FAO) in 1990 and sit on its board of trustees.[31] Supported by royalties from the family's famous toy company, the first cohort of FAO Fellows was selected in 2006. Fellows apply directly to and work for a nonprofit partner based in New York City, Philadelphia, or Boston. Each fellow serves a two-year term and divides their time between traditional internship responsibilities and a more self-directed project that contributes to the goals of their host organization while also targeting specific areas of professional development chosen by the fellow. Alongside their primary responsibilities with their host organizations, fellows participate in biannual retreats, make site visits to all of FAO's partners, and interview the partners' executive directors. Although all of the host organizations require fellows to engage in educational endeavors, only some of them are solely dedicated to education. For example, Riverkeeper, in New York City, protects the environmental, recreational, and commercial integrity of the Hudson River; and The Food Trust, headquartered in Philadelphia, works to ensure that all Americans have access to affordable, nutritious food and information about healthy eating.

Like the FAO Fellowship, the Project Horseshoe Farm Fellowship aims to foster the next generation's nonprofit leaders. Founded in 2007 as a 501(c)(3) nonprofit, Project Horseshoe Farm (PHF) launched its first community initiative in spring of that year, partnering with Greensboro (Alabama) Elementary School and the University of Alabama to provide after-school tutoring for fourth- and fifth-grade students. Two years later, PHF opened its first "Enhanced Independent Living" home to support "vulnerable" adults and senior citizens in Greensboro—a town with fewer than twenty-five hundred residents—and the surrounding communities in Hale County. Education and health care thus constitute the two primary pillars of PHF's mission.[32]

The PHF Fellowship started in 2009, when the first class of three fellows was chosen. The current cohort is comprised of fifteen fellows, chosen from colleges and universities across the country. Three members of the current class have opted to stay on for a second year, a testament to the program's value for its fellows. While many of the fellows were pre-med as undergraduates, the fellowship also attracts students interested in public policy, nonprofit management, and community development. Indeed, fellows serve the citizens of Greensboro in a variety of ways that range from providing transportation to hosting a walking club. Among its many distinct qualities, the PHF Fellowship is perhaps most unique for its emphasis on what Director John Dorsey refers to as "simple living," which requires that fellows spend half of the year living in a housing facility with no air-conditioning (in rural Alabama!), no television, and no internet access.[33]

When Karen applied for the FAO Fellowship, she was living abroad as a recipient of a prestigious fellowship. Karen was selected for her assignment as a graduating senior, and her experience turned out to be predominantly negative. Karen was especially critical of her fellowship cohort. As she joked in retrospect, her conversations with other fellows could be summed up in the following derisive terms: "We're all amazing. Let's compare our amazingness." Moreover, as her fellowship year drew to a close, Karen was disappointed by the number of her peers whom she thought were moving on robotically to the next prestigious credential.

Conversely, she found in the FAO Fellowship a like-minded cohort dedicated to the same mission. Whereas her international experience was, in Karen's words, "a little escapade for [her] to grow," she could see her impact as an FAO Fellow through her work at uAspire, a Boston-based nonprofit that helps high school students understand their financial options before enrolling in college. "I loved getting rid of the prestige," Karen reported. In this respect, she had fallen into and then escaped from the trap of credentialism, which Deresiewicz describes as the rampant belief among students at elite institutions that one's credentials "signify not just your fate, but your identity; not just your identity, but your value. They are *who* you are, and what you're worth."[34] One young person's reflections must certainly be taken with a grain of salt, but Karen's experiences pose a challenge to fellowships advisors to think more about how to identify students who can benefit from being steered away from the most prestigious opportunities to liberate themselves from the pressures and limitations of seeking credentials as an end goal. It comes back to the importance of fit. For some, the experience abroad with a particular fellowship is the right, authentic experience; for others, who may be equally capable, it is not.

Concerns about what constitutes prestige were also paramount in Rafa's journey toward the PHF Fellowship. As a graduating senior, Rafa applied for several awards, including the ETA program. When it came time to decide whether to accept her offer from the PHF Fellowship, Rafa had already heard a no from Fulbright and was still waiting on the final word from the AIF Clinton Fellowship for Service in India. Rather than continue to wait, Rafa took the plunge and accepted her PHF offer.

As a PHF Fellow, Rafa had myriad responsibilities with significant stakes—from tutoring low-income students to helping senior citizens manage their medication schedules and dietary habits—but she also had the freedom to screw up. Greensboro is a community with many needs, so fellows are given the latitude to pursue their own specific interests and develop their own projects to benefit the community. Amidst this opportunity and autonomy, Rafa told me her fellowship year made her "appreciate when things *do* go according to plan" because, perhaps for the first time, they did not.

To complement their autonomy, the fellows receive a close-knit cohort experience and tremendous mentorship from the program's director, who regularly interacts with them for two or three hours a week, typically in group settings, and who even played a weekly tennis match with Rafa while she was in Greensboro. The program has a fruitful balance of structure and autonomy, thus addressing another of Deresiewicz's chief worries. According to Deresiewicz, students' lives are excessively structured. Almost from birth, it seems, a path toward admission into an elite institution has been laid out for them, and then these institutions perpetuate the problem as students earn their degrees. "Too much structure is among the things you need to get away from," he recommends: "How about *not* enriching yourself for a change? How about doing something that you can't put on your resume (or brag about on Facebook)?"[35]

Karen enjoyed similar circumstances as an FAO Fellow. The program compels fellows to pursue an independent project within the auspices of their host organization. And just as Rafa received support from her mentor and peers, Karen received regular feedback about her performance from executive director Priscilla Cohen, who crafts and monitors the roles fellows undertake to ensure they are not just pushing paper and are instead doing fulfilling work. In both programs, then, the measure of structure and autonomy granted to fellows represents an excellent chance for them to discover who they are and what they actually want to do. Consequently, these programs address Deresiewicz's most significant diagnosis of what ails today's undergraduates: "There is an intense hunger among today's students . . . for what college ought to be providing but is not: for a larger sense of purpose and direction; for an experience at school that speaks to them as human beings, not bundles of aptitudes; for guidance in addressing the important questions of life; for simple permission to think about these things and a vocabulary with which to do so."[36]

This theme came to the fore as Rafa recounted the most surprising thing she learned about herself during her time as a PHF Fellow. The experience had revealed "weaknesses" to her, weaknesses in how she related to people and built relationships. Conversations with John Dorsey confirmed that Rafa's experience was likely a product of the fellowship's design. Dorsey contended that students from schools like Northwestern arrive in Alabama with a host of problem-solving skills—the kind of intellectual tools, he noted, that are perpetuated/exploited by the consulting gigs so many students seek—but that they lack "emotional" problem-solving skills. The PHF Fellowship challenged Rafa to think harder about who she is and what she wants to do, and therefore guided her in the lifelong project of self-authorship.

As exemplified by these programs and the benefits that accrued to Karen and Rafa through their participation in them, it is clear to us that fellowships (and fellowships advising) can play a vital part in feeding the hunger among America's undergraduates for autonomy, meaning, and self-authorship. Achieving such a result, however, requires a deliberate approach to all stages of the fellowship process—promotion, recruitment, mentoring, and celebrating applicants and recipients—to ensure that the pursuit of fellowships fosters passionate weirdos rather than excellent sheep.

Fellowships advisors, equipped with knowledge of self-authorship and the strategies of feminist pedagogy, can better leverage the fellowship process to help students find and develop their own voices and take ownership of the choices they have made, rather than continue to view their trajectories as formulas to reach externally validated markers of success. Because self-authorship may not normally even begin until someone's postgraduate years, the fellowships process is well situated to help serve this role. Importantly, the notion of self-authorship also requires that we, as advisors, embrace opportunities that may not carry the same name recognition or prestige as others, but can provide some students with the growth experiences they seek. Ultimately, fellowships require the trust of the students and the advisors that self-authorship is an intrinsic good, and that both students and society will be better for it. This, after all, is what the "college as it should be" perspective calls for: that university education, and all of the formative experiences that come with it, ultimately yields the sorts of thinkers and citizens—indeed, leaders—who will build a more just and equitable society.

Notes

1. William Deresiewicz, *Excellent Sheep: The Miseducation of the American Elite and the Way to a Meaningful Life* (New York: Free Press, 2014).

2. Richard Arum and Josipa Roksa, *Academically Adrift: Limited Learning on College Campuses* (Chicago: University of Chicago Press, 2010).

3. Jonathan Zimmerman, "Our Best and Brightest Bankers," *The Chronicle of Higher Education*, July 9, 2018.

4. Harry Boyt and Eric Fretz, "Civic Professionalism," *Journal of Higher Education Outreach and Engagement* 14, no. 2 (2010): 67–90.

5. Susan Cain, "Not Leadership Material? Good. The World Needs Followers," *The New York Times*, March 24, 2017.

6. Deresiewicz, *Excellent Sheep*, 3.

7. Arum and Roksa, *Academically Adrift*.

8. Marcia Baxter Magolda and Patricia King, "Assessing Meaning Making and Self-Authorship: Theory, Research, and Application," *ASHE Higher Education Report* 38 (2012): 3.

9. Andrew Giambrone, "I'm a Laborer's Son. I Went to Yale. I Am Not 'Trapped in a Bubble of Privilege,'" *The New Republic*, July 28, 2014.

10. Deresiewicz, *Excellent Sheep*, 136.

11. Robert Kegan, *In Over Our Heads: The Mental Demands of Modern Life* (Cambridge, MA: Harvard University Press, 1994).

12. Michael Welkener and Marcia Baxter Magolda, "Better Understanding Students' Self-Authorship via Self-Portraits," *Journal of College Student Development* 55, no. 6 (2014): 580–85. Project MUSE.

13. Marcia Baxter Magolda, "Three Elements of Self-Authorship," *Journal of College Student Development* 49, no. 4 (2008): 269–84. Project MUSE.

14. Welkener and Baxter Magolda, "Better Understanding," 581.

15. Marcia Baxter Magolda, *Making Their Own Way: Narratives for Transforming Higher Education to Promote Self-Development* (Sterling, VA: Stylus, 2001).

16. Ibid., 120.

17. Ibid.

18. Jane Pizzolato, "Developing Self-Authorship: Exploring the Experiences of High-Risk College Students," *Journal of College Student Development* 44, no. 6 (2003): 800. Project MUSE.

19. Vasti Torres and Ebelia Hernandez, "The Influence of Ethnic Identity on Self-Authorship: A Longitudinal Study of Latino/a College Students," *Journal of College Student Development* 48, no. 5 (2007): 558–73. Project MUSE.

20. Elias Abes and Susan Jones, "Meaning-Making Capacity and the Dynamics of Lesbian College Students' Multiple Dimensions of Identity," *Journal of College Student Development* 45, no. 6 (2004): 612–32. Project MUSE.

21. Marcia Baxter Magolda and Patricia King, "Toward Reflective Conversations: An Advising Approach That Promotes Self-Authorship," *Peer Review* 10, no. 1 (2008): 8–11.

22. University of Michigan, "Wabash National Study of Liberal Arts Education," https://sites.google.com/a/umich.edu/wns-qual/home.

23. University of Michigan, "Wabash National Study Interview," https://sites.google.com/a/umich.edu/wns-qual/interview-protocol.

24. University of Michigan, "Wabash National Study of Liberal Arts Education Qualitative Methods," https://sites.google.com/a/umich.edu/wns-qual/qualitative-methods.

25. Baxter Magolda and King, "Toward Reflective Conversations," 9.

26. Ibid.

27. Ibid.

28. Racquelle Bostow, Sherry Brewer, Nancy Chick, Ben Galina, Allison McGrath, Kirsten Mendoza, Kristen Navarro, and Lis Valle-Ruiz, "A Guide to Feminist Pedagogy," Vanderbilt Center for Teaching, https://my.vanderbilt.edu/femped

29. Donna Haraway, "Situated Knowledge: The Science Question in Feminism and the Privilege of Partial Perspective," *Feminist Studies* 14, no. 3 (1988): 583.

30. National Association of Fellowships Advisors, "Mission and Code of Ethics," https://nafadvisors.org/mission-and-code-ethics.

31. FAO Schwarz Fellowship, "About Us," https://faoschwarzfellowship.org/about-leadership/.

32. Project Horseshoe Farm, "Overview," https://www.projecthsf.org/overview.

33. John Dorsey (director, Project Horseshoe Farm), in discussion with the author, June 2017.

34. Deresiewicz, *Excellent Sheep*, 16.

35. Ibid., 124–5.

36. Ibid., 73.

4

You Sank My Fellowship
The "Near Miss" Truman Application

TARA YGLESIAS

Tara Yglesias has served as deputy executive secretary of the Truman Foundation for the past fifteen years and has been involved in the selection of Truman Scholars since 2001. During this time, she had the opportunity to study the trends and characteristics of each incoming class of scholars. She used this knowledge to assist in the development of new foundation programs and initiatives as well as the design of a new foundation website and online application system. An attorney by training, she began her career by spending six years in the Office of the Public Defender in Fulton County, Georgia. She specialized in trial work and serious felonies but also assisted with the training of new attorneys. A former Truman Scholar from Pennsylvania, she also served as a Senior Scholar at Truman Scholars Leadership Week and the foundation's Public Service Law Conference prior to joining the foundation's staff.

The foundation side of competitive fellowships has its frustrations. Well-meaning advice and instructions are ignored or, worse yet, interpreted in ways that strain both grammar and the space-time continuum.[1] Despite frequent warnings, absolutely everyone presses all the buttons on the application simultaneously at ten minutes to the deadline. Applicants thwart our attempts to better understand their interests by offering platitudes and vague descriptions of already confusing campus activities.[2] And while the annoying jargon might change from year to year, the frustrations they generate maintain a nice, constant level of irritation.[3]

But much like any pool of Truman applicants, there is always an overachiever. For the past several years, that frustration has been the myth of the near miss application. As fellowships advising has become more professionalized, there seems to be an increasing desire to treat competitive fellowship applications like puzzles rather than intellectual journeys. A quick scan of materials produced by members of the National Association of Fellowships Advisors (NAFA) includes myriad references to "cracking the code" and other phrasing that seems to suggest a Buzzfeed listicle rather than a sober pursuit of student growth.[4] Advisors become obsessed with the notion that if they just did *This One Thing* correctly, the outcome would be different. The application becomes a game, and too often advisors lose sight of both the application and the applicant as a whole.

There is a balance to be struck between "Top 10 Truman Must-Dos!" and an utterly holistic approach that considers the applicant's hopes and dreams but misses all the typos. This essay will explore the nuances of those applications that are close but ultimately not selected. While dispelling the myth of the "near miss," this essay will discuss the reasons why close applications are not selected. Much of the essay will focus on the process of reading and how distinctions are made, but there will also be some discussion of areas of the application where issues often occur.

Jeopardy: What Is a "Near Miss" Application?

Thanks to the increasing professionalization of advising, as well as the democratization of information on scholarships, applications are better prepared than ever. In the past decade, the number of wholly unsuitable applications has decreased to practically zero.[5] Instead we have a few brilliant applications, a few not-so-brilliant applications, and the vast majority that reside in the middle. Their individual fates can be fickle indeed. Some of these applications will advance to finalist stage; the rest will not. The reasons why one application succeeds where another fails are often difficult to articulate and certainly do not lend themselves to a pithy article. But these applications are often where the disappointment is most acute and the feedback even more important. What was the undoing of the application? How can this be avoided in the future? What should we tell the student? If this student did not succeed, how can I expect success for any of my other students?

The Truman Foundation provides feedback to advisors on applications for those students not selected for interview.[6] There is a misconception that advisors spend the time arguing their student's case and contradicting the recommendations of the panel. In nearly every case, advisors tend to be able to spot the issues with an application at least as well as our readers. Only rarely does an advisor disagree totally with the reader's assessment. But the few who do want to distill the criticism down to one specific item. Saying that "the student lacked leadership compared to the pool" is insufficient. These advisors will point to individual pieces of the application and try to debate the readers' findings. They want to know exactly when leadership is "enough" and the precise moment they[7] failed to live up to our expectations. Even those advisors who agree with our assessment often seem frustrated that we cannot point to the exact spot where the application went off the rails. These applications are what advisors consider near misses.

Providing feedback for these applications is often the most difficult. Improvements can always be made even in the applications of those selected as scholars.[8] But what should be improved is often unclear and sometimes subjective. There is never one slip that we can point to that is the difference between advancing and not. An applicant could follow every one of our #TrumanTips, an advisor could memorize every "Top 10 Truman Tips!" listicle, all the recommenders could avoid every common issue in letters of recommendation, and the application still might not be successful. These applications often fail to advance due to a mélange of choices the applicant made or larger issues involving the competitiveness of the pool.

For advisors, that explanation is often insufficient. In order to either assuage or justify the guilt of the participants, these applications must be distilled into *The One Thing* that was done wrong. General advice about the need for a compelling leadership essay gets translated into "do not write about student government." Suggestions for how best to present a case for a medical degree becomes "Truman does not fund medical degrees." The need to find something explicable—and be able to cast the blame elsewhere—is understandable. But continuing to treat the applications as if there are simple pitfalls to avoid leaves the student playing Application Whack-a-Mole: each time they are successful in removing an issue (not writing about medical school), another pops up (all of their service and academics are geared toward a degree in medicine). The end result is an application that ticks off the boxes but is denuded of any sense of what really drives the student. Even worse, the growth that the student could have from honestly completing the application is curtailed in an effort to avoid pitfalls.

Wheel of Application Misfortune

Truman applications are initially reviewed by a twenty-one-member Finalist Selection Committee (FSC). Applicants are grouped into regions by state of residence and given to teams for reading. Each three-person team spends an average of fifteen minutes per application. Every application is read twice; close or controversial applications are read three times.[9] Weak applications are removed, strong applications are advanced, and then the readers must deal with the vast majority of applications in the middle. Readers often have double or triple the number of close applications than they do spots for interviews. The difference between advancing and not advancing is slim.

There are three reasons why an application does not advance from the reading stage:

1. The Pool
2. Reader Malfunction
3. Application Malfunction

Readers are instructed to advance the top eleven candidates in each region. They are told explicitly not to consider:

- *State of residence.* The top applicants are advanced regardless of where they reside.

- *School affiliation.* Other than the general limit on nominations, there is no limit on how many students from a school can advance in the competition.
- *Subject matter.* Readers can advance as many applicants with the same topic as they wish.[10]
- *Degree program.* Other than a prohibition against MBAs, the foundation does not set a degree-funding priority.

This list is not exhaustive, but these items are often suggested by advisors as reasons why their students do not advance. In reality, the reasons why some applications do not advance are a bit more difficult to identify and prevent.

Go Fish: The Truman Applicant Pool

The applicant pool is the barrier to advancement for most applications. The difference in competitiveness of a region from one cycle to the next can be significant. One year's standout can be the next cycle's wallflower. More disconcertingly, it is nearly impossible to guess which regions might be most competitive in a given year. Given that students can generally apply from both their home address and their school address,[11] it is even difficult to determine which institutions are likely to provide applicants in a given year. Absent some sort of Godfather-esque vendetta against the other nominees, there is nothing to be done to dilute the strength of the pool. While increasingly infrequent, we sometimes have applications that are in the wrong pool. Truman is often seen as a stepping-stone for other competitive fellowships. A student can be a good candidate for both Truman and another competitive fellowship, but there are also outstanding, compelling candidates who do not fit the Truman program—a student who has academic excellence and research experience, but little sense of how to translate that into compelling public policy, or a student who has leadership skills, but seems to lack an interest in public service. These students may score well in the evaluation process, but are ultimately not selected for interview because our readers conclude they are "not a Truman." While this might suggest that advisors can identify these students early and not put them forward, the reality is quite different.[12] There is no way to tell what a pool looks like in a given year. The lone researcher or public service neophyte might merit an interview in a year where the pool is less strong.

In either case, the pool can keep an otherwise good candidate from advancing. Feedback will provide suggestions on ways to improve, but even if these suggestions had been followed, the application would likely not have advanced. Prevention is not an option. The best tactic to deal with the pool is both make sure the student is aware of the competitive nature of the application process and emphasize the growth that comes from diligently participating in the process. Even something as mundane as having a start on graduate school applications can be compelling for some students and provide some comfort if the pool keeps them from advancing. For the more "evolved" students, a focus on the growth that comes from exploring the ideas in the application itself can provide solace in the event the application does not advance.

Concentration: The Truman Application Reader

An infrequent, but still significant, cause of an application not advancing is reader malfunction. When tasking a human to do a lengthy, repetitive, yet subjective task that requires intense concentration but takes place amid plentiful food and warm ambient room temperatures, mistakes sometimes happen. Readers may give an application too little attention and miss the student's myriad achievements or give the application too much attention and be overly or unnecessarily critical. Sometimes applicants may be the unlucky victim of a shuffle that has their application being read immediately after the candidate who will go on to win Truman, Rhodes & Marshall, the MacArthur Genius Grant, and the Fields Medal before their eventual EGOT, and they suffer in comparison. It could happen that an applicant gets read immediately after something made the reader upset.[13] Even with their professional detachment, formidable stamina, and extensive training, our readers are human. It is a subjective process. Hence each application is read by multiple humans.

Aside from the obvious advice of ensuring that the application is thoughtful and precise, the best way to control for reader error is through the appeals process. Schools are permitted to appeal one student not selected for interview to be reread by a second appeals committee. Information about the process is in the emails sent at the end of the selection cycle.

Advisors are strongly encouraged to take advantage of the appeals process. The foundation's stated position is that any file is eligible for review on appeal. The foundation does not keep records of how frequently an institution requests appeals or the success rate of those appeals, so foregoing an appeal in an effort to save political capital for future years is not necessary. Additionally, it is virtually impossible for an advisor to be able to tell how close an application was to advancing, so a decision not to appeal might not be based on the best information. Appeals are not considered a second round of selection with lower expectations; these applicants are treated the same as any other once they are selected on appeal.[14] Students are not told of the appeals process unless they are selected for interview.[15] Some faculty have told their applicants about the process as a way to underscore that their application received thorough consideration. Focusing on this aspect may be helpful for some students while others might benefit from the finality of the process without discussing appeals.

Scattergories: Application Issues

Both a competitive pool and a potentially error-prone reader might be exacerbated by significant issues in the application. Significant is the key term in this case: these issues are not ones that can be corrected by adhering to a checklist.

Readers simply cannot determine when application issues are the result of a true lack of experience or an inability to effectively present those experiences. Readers are instructed to let the application make the case for itself—they are not to fill in blanks for students or give them the benefit of the doubt when responses are unclear.[16] While the sections below assume a deficiency in the application, several applications each year do not advance because applicants cannot effectively discuss their experiences.

The foundation encourages students to begin the Truman process early, in part because it helps position them for experiences necessary to be successful as a future public service leader, but also because students rarely have the ability to write well and present themselves clearly without a significant amount of time to review and reflect. Those who are serious about competitive fellowships and graduate school, particularly those students who come from backgrounds and majors where writing is not emphasized, need practice at establishing their voice. Even those students with robust writing backgrounds or innate skill need to unlearn academic writing in order to produce a more effective Truman application.[17]

Ticket to Ride: Establishing Leadership

Leadership is evaluated by considering the applicant's list of activities[18] as well as their response to Question 7 ("a specific example of your leadership") and supporting letters. Successful applications tend to exude leadership in other areas of the application as well, including in the service experience (Question 8) as well as the ambition in their career plans.

Truman has always had a somewhat nontraditional notion of leadership. Those students who merely occupy positions of authority, even impressive ones, are not necessarily leaders. Leaders are those who either take an existing leadership position and do something innovative with it or those who create their own leadership position around an issue of interest to them. As such, leadership experiences must be unique to the student. If any one of several students from a given organization could write the same essay, that probably means the student was not innovative with their leadership position. We also tend to moderate what we expect from students based on what we know of the student's ambition and personality. Truman has different leadership requirements for students who lead through consensus in small-scale groups and plan for a career in that type of field than we do for students who express a desire to occupy a position of national leadership where controversy will be a daily occurrence.

With that leadership definition as a backdrop, there are three common issues in the leadership portion of the application. Each will come with an example of what readers see during the review.[19]

1. **Guess Who?** "*In weekly meetings, we planned a series of public events to make the issue more visible and to stimulate student interest. We developed and executed a detailed action plan, but I will share none of the details here. We did a lot of other things, perhaps individually, perhaps as a group. You will never know. I'm going to close without any data or clear indication of what anyone did individually.*"

    Assuming it is not a nod to all things Truman, this issue of giving credit to others to the detriment of their own application seems to plague the Truman process.[20]

This tendency is probably a function of what draws the applicants to service in the first place. While sharing credit is an admirable trait, it often leaves readers confused. Additionally, more and more organizations are eschewing traditional leadership structures, so it is doubly difficult to tell how much leadership is required of students if they will not explain themselves.

Readers only have the student's words to understand and evaluate the activity, and readers are likely unfamiliar with the student's campus and only passingly familiar with their campus organization. Assuming that a reader will intuitively understand how important a role the applicant plays is risky. Applicants should be clear about their roles, the size of the student organization as well as its reach. This territory may be uncomfortable for students not used to basking in the limelight, but it is necessary for readers to understand the level of leadership involved.[21]

2. **Apples to Apples:** *"As a residence hall leader, I was responsible for answering student questions and organizing one information session a month. Once, I did one on recycling. In my mind, our campaign to raise awareness of recycling was a success. Yes, I know I had a very interesting internship listed in Question 4 that probably had a better leadership example in it. No, I'm not going to talk much about it."*

Readers usually do not find campus enrichment activities—Model UN, debate, and, to a lesser extent, residence hall leadership, and student government—very compelling unless there is substantial leadership that is likely to translate into real-world skills. Engaging a captive audience of dorm room dwellers on campus issues is not nearly as impressive as shepherding that group through a time of controversy or crisis. That is not to say each leadership example needs to hinge on dramatic events, but it is helpful if there is a narrative arc of sorts. "I did a good job as SGA president" is not a narrative arc.

The problem with these activities is that they can be very, very time-consuming, but often do not serve to do much other than enrich the applicant's skill set. These sorts of activities often engage an already engaged group of students around an activity that is necessarily closed to other people. If students can find a way to use a campus organization to reach out to others beyond the organization or create change around an issue for a greater good, it is perfectly appropriate for a leadership essay. Unfortunately, the bulk of essays around such activities do not meet these criteria.

Emphasizing the service to others might be helpful. Most of our applications have leadership examples that reach beyond a small campus group. In comparison, a student whose sole leadership involves successfully shepherding their debate team can seem more self-serving and will not be as compelling. Having students look at the application as early as possible allows them to get an idea of where their application might be lacking.[22]

Interestingly, students often have other items in their applications that would prove more compelling. Just because an activity is time-consuming does not make it the best leadership example. Additionally, difficulty in getting a supporting letter is not a reason not to write about a leadership activity. A supporting letter is nice, but a letter that just mentions the activity can be perfectly acceptable. But please interpret this advice as narrowly as possible.

Finally, there really is no hierarchy of leadership activities. But readers often give feedback that draws a distinction between those activities they find compelling—where an applicant's organization, no matter how small or how specific an issue area, leads people on campus or in the community—and those they do not, where an applicant manages to organize a group of people already involved in an activity to improve things for themselves.

3. **Connect Four:** *"Please allow me to shoehorn in an activity from high school that I would like to mention. You will emerge confused as to the time frame of those efforts and what my current interests are."*

Readers put far greater stock in recent activities. An upward trend in leadership and service is often rewarded with an interview. But sometimes applicants, particularly nontraditional students, have significant leadership from before college. For those students it can be a struggle to present those items well in the application.

In general, overstuffing Question 7 is not the best way to

ensure readers credit earlier leadership. If the leadership example is ongoing (perhaps the student started an organization in high school that they continue to lead), then the essay can have a longer-term focus. But in that case, students need to be clear about the timeline and to focus the essay on recent events even if there is more compelling leadership in the past. Those experiences can be discussed in detail in either the supporting letter of recommendation or in Question 14 (additional information).

Likewise, applicants who have several leadership activities around the same issue sometimes try to include all relevant experiences in one essay. Providing the readers with sufficient detail for more than one activity is nearly impossible given the space constraints of this essay. Readers want to see the applicant's leadership in detail on one specific issue. The overview belongs in the letter of recommendation.

Chutes and Ladders: Power Dynamics in the Truman Application

The Nominee Rating Form contains the rather dry phrase "Appropriateness for proposed graduate study."[23] While that category includes our only reference to the transcript, the main purpose is to evaluate how the applicant understands power.[24] Readers will still sometimes refer to this characteristic as an applicant's "change agent potential," but business schools seem to have co-opted that phrase beyond all meaning.

Power in the Truman application is both about how the applicant plans to accumulate power and what they plan to do with power once they have it. Both components need to be in evidence for a successful application. Leadership, as described above, goes a long way to establishing that the applicant understands how to gain power. But the readers also need to see a clear plan for the next steps.

After applicants have established their areas of interest, the readers then look to their graduate school plans (Question 11) as well as their career goals (Question 12 for immediate employment after graduate school, Question 13 for five to seven years later) to see if the applicants have an understanding for how best to gather power in their chosen area. The applicant should show both an understanding of the needed academic credentials and the role intangible elements like network building, institutional prestige, and early career development opportunities play in the development of a power base.

From there, readers look to see what applicants plan to do with the power they have accumulated. It is not enough for an applicant to build an impressive resume; they need to also show that they plan to make a difference beyond burnishing their credentials. Readers look to Questions 12 and 13 to see not only a trajectory of leadership, but also a plan for change. The evaluation of these responses is very dependent on the applicant's interests as the reader understands them. It is important both that applicants clearly explain their interests and that their understanding of power is level with those interests. So an applicant with mostly local political involvement would be expected to accumulate and expend power in different ways from someone who aspires to being a player on the international stage.

But much like taking sole credit for leadership opportunities, Truman applicants also struggle to admit to their own ambitions. Convincing applicants that it is okay to admit to being ambitious can be a significant step forward. But the power dynamics of the Truman application can bump up against all sorts of other issues—imposter syndrome, a lack of quality mentoring, writing difficulties—so that it becomes imperative that the applicant at least accepts that power is a concept worth embracing. From there, applicants can work on mastering how they express their need for and use of power.

> **Mystery Date:** *"Harvard, the most prestigious graduate school in the country, is my choice for a law degree. Please allow me to tediously list the required coursework." or "I plan to work for the Department of Justice in the Office of Extremely Long Names That Actually Don't Provide Much Information and Federal Programs. I shall provide no other information as to my ambitions."*

The purpose of these questions is to get a better understanding of students' ambitions and determine if they have a clear idea of how best to impact the issues that concern them. While part of that includes a clear statement of which graduate school is best for them and where they would like to work, an extremely detailed view of either is unnecessary.

The readers know a great deal about both graduate schools and public service career paths. Telling them that contracts is a required first-year course for law students does not come as a revelation. What does prove to be revelatory is an understanding of how applicants will transition from the graduate school plan of their choice to their first career. The applicant's ambition and understanding of their own skills is on display here. For some students, this section can reveal gaps in their knowledge or a mis-understanding of the skills needed to work on an issue. For others, it can reveal a lack of confidence in their own abilities.

Applicants should understand that these questions are not about who comes up with the best plan, but instead what is the best plan for them. Winning applications have proposed attending the top graduate school programs as well as programs that are relatively unknown. Some appli-cants propose getting right into the fray, while others are content with more measured growth. But for successful applicants, these questions reveal applicants' understanding of how best to credential themselves and then position themselves to have an impact.

Advising matters. The difference between an applicant who has access to good advising and those who do not is often marked. Encourage appli-cants to talk to people in the field other than professors. Aside from pro-viding good practice in talking to adults, it will give applicants more career trajectories to choose from as well as the confidence to write about the path they have chosen.

1. **Stratego:** *"After five to seven years of working on behalf of the Department of State, I hope to be promoted to the Next Level of Bureaucracy. That is all. Thank you."*

   Fortunately for the country, countless applicants each year want to dedicate their service to the bureaucratic institutions that probably contribute to the very problems they wish to address. Unfortunately for their applications, this dedication often makes for an unsatisfying essay.

   Readers still expect to see leadership and an understanding of how change is made even when a student plans to work within an existing system that may be resistant to change. Applicants in these professions need to make a point of acknowledging the difficulties they will face, lest they appear naive. Speaking with someone in the field may prove helpful if only to assure the applicant that change is still possible.

Most applicants will not have a lot of space to discuss their understanding of the power dynamics in their bureaucracy of choice, but they should likely temper their stated ambitions to be appropriate to the office. Applicants may also choose to write a policy proposal for the same agency and thus have more room to display their understanding of the political nuances of working for an entrenched bureaucracy. Letters of recommendation can be very helpful in this area. Recommenders who are familiar with the institutions the applicant plans to work with can provide needed context.

2. **Clue:** *"I realize at no point have I mentioned an interest in children, which is why I plan a career in K–12 education."*

With the fixation on near misses comes a tendency to focus on parts of the application rather than the whole of the application. Each essay might be a work of persuasive genius but may still not give an overall picture of the applicant. At a minimum, the application reads as a disjointed series of accomplishments. But more often, it appears that the applicant does not understand the importance of experience.

These types of applications generally fall into two specific categories. The first is areas of interest where it is difficult to have relevant experience, particularly depending on the location of the applicant's institution. Applicants at a small liberal arts college in the Midwest may have a difficult time gaining direct, relevant experience in security or intelligence issues, for instance. But even in those cases, there are activities that relate to applicants' career goals that would allow them to demonstrate an understanding about how to have an impact on the issues of concern to them. The experiences can be classroom based, in a related field, or through internships. For areas where direct experience is impossible, the application becomes about the student's persistence and understanding that experience is an important component of gathering power.

The other category is experience that should be fairly easy

to come by, but, for whatever reason, an applicant chooses not to gain that experience. This situation occurs most often in two areas: education and poverty. Readers tend to react negatively to those applicants who plan a career in poverty research without ever seeming to have met poor people, or those who plan to revamp education policy without ever having been around children. Convincing readers that an interest is sincerely held is difficult when an applicant cannot be bothered to have at least some experience in the two most abundant types of campus service activities available. Applicants should demonstrate that, in addition to their formidable intellect, they have an understanding of the human components of their issue.

In both instances, applicants should take care not to frame their experiences narrowly. A campus activity that requires discretion and consensus building on the part of applicants can demonstrate that they have the capability to work in a sensitive field like intelligence. Likewise, a volunteer program with school-aged children can demonstrate that an applicant is more than a heartless, number-crunching bureaucrat. Applicants can use Question 8 (a significant public service experience) to tease out these connections and provide the reader with the assurance that they understand the power dynamics of their issue.

3. **Dominion:** *"I plan to run for office because I believe that to whom much is given, much is required. When I am elected, I plan to ensure that we are a nation of laws, solving a variety of social ills. I will now communicate my plan in vague phrases."*

There are certain applicants who inherently understand power. They have accumulated power since arriving on campus and often use it for good. But they can lack a clear vision of how to use that power. These applications are usually marked by a feeling that applicants are being buffeted from one issue to another, the only connection being that it was a place where they had power and could exert it.

Applicants who struggle to write Question 9 (describe a problem or need of society you want to address) often fall into this category. Their responses to Question 9 are often vague in telltale ways, relying on hoary phrasing and general discussions of issues like civil rights or inequality. These applicants may also struggle with Questions 11 (graduate school) and 12 (career immediately following graduate school) because they are focused on the end goal of elected office.

That is not to say these applicants are not appropriate for Truman. But they do require a check on their heretofore unchecked power. Not that the worry is a turn to public service despotism, but an application with an understanding of power but without any relevant values ensures the applicant will seem a cipher to readers.

For these applicants, a little soul-searching is in order. They need to reflect on why they are interested in accumulating power, and how they have used it in the past. Generally, there is some issue in which they are most engaged. That issue may be as vague as "political engagement," but at least that is a possible foundation for the application. These applications often benefit from reads by people who do not know them or their work well. Such readers can often point out when applicants have become a bundle of ambition versus when they are conveying their values as well as their understanding of power.

The Game of Life: Bringing the Application Together

Perhaps the reason why those "Top 10 Truman Tips" lists are so appealing is that they make pulling the application together seem easy. Just check for these few items, make sure public always has an "I" in it, and success is guaranteed! The reality is much more nuanced.

Advisors will never be able to control the strength of the pool in a given cycle. Advisors will never be able to ensure every application reader is well-fed and cheerful when they read an application. Advisors cannot fix a student who writes imprecisely or refuses to put in the necessary time to make a successful application. Advisors cannot will a student to have the necessary leadership to advance or the understanding of power to make their application stand out. Even if an advisor identifies a problem with an application and the applicant is inclined to fix it, most of these issues cannot be sorted with a quick redraft.

But what advisors can do is use the application as a tool. Early identification of potential applicants means they will have more time to develop leadership skills and understand the realm in which they want to make a difference. It also means that the applicants can have more conversations about the work they love, and that can lead to internships, volunteer experiences, jobs, and other new opportunities. Applicants can take the time to improve their writing, something that will pay dividends throughout their careers. For many applicants, even those not selected for interview, the process of the Truman application is transformative in determining their path in public service. Applicants think not just about the end goal but how to get there and what experiences to have along the way.

It is not easy abandoning the notion that these applications are games to be won, and that readers can be defeated with the right assortment of tips and cheat codes.[25] But moving away from the "near miss" and toward a holistic view of the application makes for both better applications and more enriched applicants. And that is a Yahtzee.

Notes

1. I once had a student try to convince me that our allowance for early graduation did not apply to the student because "early" is a relative term.

2. As much as I enjoyed the recent film *Spider-Man: Into the Spider-Verse*, all I could think about was how many "with great power comes great responsibility" quotations I would be seeing this cycle.

3. Once the term *change agent* made its way into the world of venture capitalism, we were in for trouble.

4. I am just as guilty as anyone. I once gave a presentation entitled "Common Truman Mistakes in 10 Minutes or Less or Your Pizza is Free!" To be fair, I was only given ten minutes.

5. This category of application would include those that are incomplete or filled out in such a way that it is apparent neither the student nor the advisor reads any materials relating to selection. As recently as a decade ago, these applications comprised about 10 percent of our total applicant pool.

6. Annually this translates into feedback on approximately 150 of the 600 files not selected for interview. The feedback process begins after scholars are announced and continues roughly until the next application launches (April to August).

7. I am leaving "they" deliberately vague as it is often unclear whether the advisor feels this issue was a failing of their student or of their advising.

8. Consider this my annual warning about using successful applications as

samples for future applicants. Some Truman Scholars were selected *in spite of* their materials, and advisors cannot know which scholars those might be.

9. A controversial application would be split decisions where one reader votes to advance and the other does not. There is no subject matter or activity that would be deemed controversial by our selection panels. We have indeed seen everything.

10. There is likewise no assessment by the readers as to whether an issue is important or not. If the student finds an issue compelling, the issue is compelling enough to advance. We do not rank or suggest topics suitable for advancement.

11. Residence for the Truman is demonstrated by meeting two of these three options: 1. Home address for school registration (most schools have both a family home and a local address on file for a student); 2. Parent's home address; and 3. Place of registration to vote. For students who choose to vote from their school address, they can now have some flexibility about the state they choose.

12. We also recognize that there are sometimes external pressures to nominate certain specific or specific types of students. If this issue persists on a particular campus, the advisor may wish to invite a Truman representative for a visit or videoconference to discuss our criteria.

13. We often read the applications over Valentine's Day weekend. Do with that information what you will.

14. The fact that an application is selected on appeal is not transmitted to the interview committee. Once appeals files are added to the interview pool, the designation is removed, and the file is treated the same as any other.

15. The foundation has attempted to keep the appeals process from candidates in an effort to prevent lobbying for the institution's appeals slot. Much like any good secret, however, most applicants are aware of the process. Advisors may need to consider how and whether to discuss the appeals process with their candidates.

16. The actual reader instructions tell them not to make the case for the student, that is why we have appeals.

17. Students have, for the most part, been working in a writing format where brevity is not prized. Just getting them to stop the bloat is a huge step. After that, we will work on jargon and clichés.

18. Questions 2 (campus activities), 3 (community service activities), 4 (government activities).

19. Actual responses and reader critiques can be found at https://www.truman.gov/effective-and-ineffective-responses.

20. One of the Harry Truman quotations the foundation often emblazons on t-shirts is: "It is amazing what you can accomplish if you do not care who gets the credit." Excellent life advice translates into ineffective application advice.

21. For those thinking it will be covered in a letter of recommendation, keep

in mind that the application is read first. Readers could make up their minds about the level of leadership before ever getting to the letters. Also, readers are specifically instructed that the letters are to confirm, not supplant what is in the application.

22. Speaking—slowly!—as a former intercollegiate debater, a big wake-up call was looking at graduate school applications and realizing that if I stuck with debate, I would have one activity to write about.

23. A copy can be found here: https://www.truman.gov/nominee-rating -form.

24. Thanks to Dr. Andy Rich, former executive secretary of the foundation, for giving this category a much punchier name (even if he did want to talk about power all the time).

25. This is a game reference, not a suggestion that we take a foray into academic dishonesty.

Part II

Best Practices for Advisors and Advising Offices

5

Gender and the Characterization of Leadership in Recommendations for Nationally Competitive Awards

PAULA WARRICK

With Contributions From Ketevan Mamiseishvili, Andrew Rich, Patricia Scroggs, And Jane Curlin

---

Paula Warrick, as senior director of American University's Office of Merit Awards, oversees the university's efforts to mentor candidates for nationally competitive scholarships. She has nineteen years of professional experience in this field and has been an active member of NAFA. She served as the organization's fourth president and recently co-organized a NAFA regional workshop on national scholarships as vehicles for engaging in public service. Warrick has received an American University Staff Award for Outstanding Performance and an Alice Paul Award, which recognizes AU staff, alumni, and faculty for their commitment to continuing the suffragist leader's vision for women's equality. Paula Warrick holds a PhD in art history and taught European art for more than fifteen years.

Jane Curlin *is director of Education Programs with the Morris K. and Stewart L. Udall Foundation. Between 1994 and 1998, she was the Truman Scholarship faculty representative and director of nationally competitive scholarships at the University of Tulsa. She has a PhD in English from the University of Tulsa.*

Ketevan Mamiseishvili *is associate dean for Academic and Student Affairs and professor of higher education in the College of Education and Health Professions. She joined the University of Arkansas in August 2008 after completing her PhD in educational leadership and policy analysis at the University of Missouri.*

Andrew Rich *has served as executive secretary of the Truman Scholarship Foundation since 2011. Before joining the foundation, he was president and CEO of the Roosevelt Institute, a nonprofit organization devoted to carrying forward the legacy and values of Franklin and Eleanor Roosevelt. He has recently accepted a new position as dean of the Colin Powell School for Civic and Global Leadership at The City College of New York. He has a PhD in political science from Yale University.*

Patricia Scroggs *is director of Diplomatic Fellowships at Howard University, where she oversees administration of the Charles B. Rangel International Affairs Program and the Thomas R. Pickering Foreign Affairs Fellowship (beginning in 2019). She is a retired State Department Foreign Service Officer and has led the Rangel program since 2006.*

Does gendered language appear in recommendations for applicants for nationally competitive merit scholarships, and what is the potential impact on female candidates if so? Past studies have explored the characterization of women applicants as scholars in references for faculty and postdoctoral research positions. These analyses point to the existence of gender schema in such letters and raise important questions about the relationship between references and access to selective academic positions.

National scholarships provide an interesting opportunity to assess the applicability of such findings to other contexts. These competitions take a broad view of merit, defining it to include not just academic excellence, but also leadership, a commitment to a designated career path, and perseverance in the face of adversity. For this reason, they allow one to examine whether patterns of language that appear in letters for faculty or postdoctoral fellowship positions, often in relation to the candidate's potential to make an original scholarly contribution, also appear in letters for opportunities where nonacademic qualities are an important factor in selection.

The clear and public nature of the selection criteria for these awards offers an added incentive to undertake such an analysis. Most if not all of these awards are named for a distinguished individual, almost always a man. Each one has a distinct ethos and benefits from branding aimed at honoring the namesake's legacy or burnishing his reputation. As an important form of branding, the scholarship selection criteria are generally well thought-out and widely disseminated by means of mission statements, published selection criteria, and scholar profiles. Due to their clarity, reviewers can assess whether there is a disconnect between the aspirational scholar, as conveyed by the selection criteria, and real women candidates, as portrayed in references intended to help lift them into these opportunities.

My motivation to explore this issue began in 2016 when I came across a study pointing to gender differences in recommendations for postdoctoral fellowships within the discipline of earth sciences.[1] Wanting to know how broadly applicable the authors' findings were, I began asking the directors of prominent national scholarship programs for their insights. Because they have an imperative to cultivate future leaders of America, in addition to strong students, I chose to focus on public service-oriented awards. The directors of the Rangel, Truman, and Udall scholarship programs agreed to review letters submitted for their competitions and, ultimately, to join me in presenting their findings at the NAFA Biennial Meeting in Philadelphia in July 2017. I am grateful to Patricia Scroggs, Andy Rich, and Jane Curlin for their contributions to that panel and to this essay.

Teaming up with Ketevan Mamiseishvili for a Women's Academic Leadership Workshop at the University of Arkansas in June 2018 provided a welcome opportunity to continue this investigation. I am indebted to Professor Mamiseishvili for her thought-provoking analysis of the existing literature on gender bias in letters of recommendation, an updated version of which appears in this article. I would also like to acknowledge the work of my colleague at American University, Professor Lauren Weis, who joined Patricia Scroggs, Andy Rich, and me for a preliminary session on this topic in January 2017 at American University's Ann Ferren Teaching Conference. She introduced us to key literature on references and evaluated it through the lens of gender studies.

Gender Differences in Recommendation Letters

Research has revealed gender differences in recommendation letters written for male and female applicants for a variety of fields and positions. Trix and Psenka (2003) conducted one of the earlier studies that examined these differences.[2] They reviewed 312 letters of recommendation that were submitted between 1992 and 1995 for medical faculty positions and concluded that the letters written for women applicants were shorter and more likely to include doubt raisers and stereotypical language. More specifically, 24 percent of the letters for women included a doubt raiser (e.g., negative language, irrelevant information, faint praise, or hedges) compared to only 12 percent of letters written for men. Additionally, letters for men focused on research, skills, and abilities versus letters for female applicants that made references to their teaching, training, and application. Recommenders were also more generous in their use of standout adjectives (e.g., excellent, outstanding, exceptional, etc.) when they described male applicants compared to female applicants who were more frequently characterized in grindstone terms (e.g., hardworking, thorough, conscientious, meticulous, etc.).

More recent studies confirmed some of these findings. Schmader, Whitehead, and Wysocki (2007) concluded that the recommendation letters for female job applicants for chemistry and biochemistry faculty positions used significantly more grindstone words as compared to male applicants, whose letters contained more standout adjectives.[3] Another study that reviewed 624 letters written for psychology faculty positions showed that letters for female applicants contained more doubt raisers than letters for men, including negative language, hedging, and faint praise. The differences in the tone of the letter emerged irrespective of the country of origin. The review of 1,224 letters from fifty-four countries written for postdoctoral fellowships in geosciences found that female applicants were half less likely to receive excellent versus good letters.[4] In other words, letters written for men often referred to the applicants as "a top-notch scientist," "a scientific leader," or "superior to other students."[5]

Female applicants are less likely to be described as future leaders in the field or someone who shows leadership potential according to a study by Hoffman, Grant, McCormick, Jezewski, Matemavi, and Langnas (2018).[6] Of the 311 recommendation letters in Hoffman et al.'s (2018) study, 7.5 percent of the letters written for female applicants included the phrase "future leader" as opposed to 16.1 percent for male applicants. The letters were also less likely to describe women with attributes commonly associated with the leader. Hoffman et al.'s (2018) review found that the letters for men more frequently included words with agentic orientation, such as "dominant, confident, solid and exceptional."[7] The differences in the tone of the letters that described a candidate as "game changer" or "best in show" on the one hand and "achieves without drama" or "upbeat, fun loving" on the other were not hard to miss.[8]

The use of agentic versus communal adjectives was also the focus of the investigation conducted by Madera, Hebl, and Martin (2009).[9] In this study, the letter writers often used communal terms, such as nurturing, interpersonal, or caring to describe female applicants for early-career faculty positions in psychology. In comparison, agentic adjectives were used in reference to male applicants, who were described as ambitious, confident, or assertive. Recommendations for female applicants also often made references to their social-communal role and talked about their family or children, or them as students and colleagues.

Some may say that these are subtle differences depicting the gendered schemas and roles that exist in society. Women and men even highlight different personal qualities and skills when they describe themselves in their own personal statements.[10] However, such disparities build "over time to provide men with more advantages than women."[11] Thus, even subtle differences in the letter tone are troublesome, especially in light of the absence of objective variabilities in qualifications and productivity.

Research has shown that gender bias in recommendation letters exists even when the studies control for measures of productivity.[12] In the absence of objective differences in qualifications and achievement, the letters still reveal implicit bias that cannot be overlooked. Additionally, evidence from research suggests that differences in the tone and language of letters affect hiring decisions. Madera et al. (2009) found a negative relationship between the use of communal adjectives and hiring decisions.[13] Similarly, even slight negativity in letters raised concerns. Madera et al.'s recent study (2018) concluded that having even one doubt raiser in the letter led to significantly lower ratings of the applicant.[14]

There is potentially some good news that is worth noting. Hoffman et al. (2018) found that the letters of recommendation written from 2012 to 2017 were significantly less likely to describe male candidates in agentic terms compared to the letters written during an earlier time frame of 2006–2011. Additionally, full professors and division chiefs seemed more likely to characterize female transplant surgery applicants in their letters using communal adjectives. This could suggest that over time the differences in the language may decline. The use of standardized letter of evaluation templates may also help alleviate gender bias in recommendations. A recent study that examined the narrative statements of the standardized letter of evaluation for 1,025 emergency medicine residency applicants showed no difference in the negative language and even found that ability words referencing applicants' intelligence and skills were more frequently used to describe female candidates.[15] The use of a standardized prompt that asks the recommender to summarize and highlight specific skills or attributes of an applicant in a concise format does seem to make a difference.

Leadership as an Essential Criterion for Public Service–Oriented Scholarships

Leadership does not have a single definition, but in the context of public service–oriented scholarships, the term often refers to the candidate's potential to transform society in service to the public good. The mission statement of the Rangel Fellowship notes the program's desire for "individuals interested in helping to shape a freer, more secure and prosperous world through formulating, representing, and implementing U.S.

foreign policy."[16] The Truman Foundation urges prospective applicants to ask themselves whether they "hope to be a 'change agent,' in time, improving the ways that government agencies, nonprofit organizations, or educational institutions serve the public."[17] The Udall Foundation aspires to "strengthen Native nations, assist federal agencies and others to resolve environmental conflicts, and to encourage the continued use and appreciation of our nation's rich resources."[18] The desired candidate is "working towards positive solutions to environmental challenges or to issues impacting Indian country" and can "inspire and motivate others to take action."[19] In all three cases, the scholarships valorize assertiveness and agency, by using action-oriented verbs and terms such as "change agent" to characterize their model applicant.

Characterizations of Leadership in Letters of Recommendation

There is no evidence that, collectively, letters of recognition fail to make a case for women applicants' leadership in these three competitions. Women are not underrepresented in scholarship outcomes; in fact, the reverse is true. Patricia Scroggs notes that about two-thirds of both applicants and recipients to the Rangel Fellowship program are women, citing as factors women's higher college attendance and study abroad rates, as well as their level of academic attainment. Similarly, 60 to 70 percent of Truman applicants and new scholars have been women in recent years, a statistic matched by the Udall Scholarship competition.

Women may not outperform men in terms of the quality of their recommendations, however. The three program directors were able to identify letters that described female candidates in terms that downplayed or even undercut their leadership in relation to the selection criteria. When passages the program directors singled out as problematic are read together, patterns of representation emerge that reinforce findings in studies of letters for faculty and postdoctoral fellowship positions. In the letters excerpted below, candidates' names have been changed and some phrasing has been modified in order to ensure the anonymity of the applicant and the referee.

The directors noted the use of gender schema or gendered adjectives to describe female applicants' greatest strengths of character in some letters. Thus, we learn that "Jane has outstanding interpersonal skills and empathy and makes others around her feel comfortable" and that another applicant "is a joy to have in class—enthusiastic, constructive, thoughtful, and in the end appreciative. She is pleasant and organized."

As Patricia Scroggs observes, some gendered language may be compatible with aspects of the leadership criteria of public service–oriented scholarships. The Rangel program cultivates future diplomats, a profession that benefits from traditionally "female" traits such as consensus building, interpersonal skills, and cultural competency. Similarly, the Udall Scholarship prioritizes "civility and consensus-building" as central to the conflict resolution work it promotes. When the letter writer describes such qualities well and connects them to clear outcomes that mesh well with the scholarship's mission, the reference is an asset to the candidate. For example:

> During her study abroad experience in Japan, Rachel formed close ties with Japanese and other international students and was able to found an English language speaking club. This required her to show outstanding initiative, as well as interpersonal and cross-cultural skills. . . . Her efforts were all the more impressive in a society where women often do not take leadership roles. Her ability to navigate cultural differences, as well as her flexibility in tailoring her approach to be effective in this context, indicate an individual who will be a highly effective diplomat.

Problems arise when a candidate's civility, respectfulness, and peace-building skills come across in a letter as a matter of docility or tractability. Some references undermined the applicant by describing her in terms that might characterize a very good administrative assistant. We learn that "Becky is honest, polite, and hard-working. Additionally, she impressed us with her work ethic and ability to perform successfully even on the most mundane of administrative tasks. We counted on her ability to perform those duties which senior staff neglect and often fall through the cracks. She always did so with a smile!" At times, such comments are clearly incompatible with the candidate's role within the organization. "Jade is a charming, soft-spoken, and deeply respectful young woman, who has lived and served abroad as a U.S. Marine," commented one referee.

In a few notable cases, the tendency to evaluate women for their interpersonal and consensus-building skills fed into a form of racial stereotyping in which members of certain minority groups are depicted as nasty, aggressive, or resentful in response to perceived mistreatment. A few of the

letters the program directors singled out for discussion evoke images of stereotypical types, such as "the angry black woman" or "the fierce Latina."
One referee noted that a female candidate "is involved extensively with the
campus chapter of Black Lives Matter, but she is nevertheless polite and
respectful of authority." In contrast, "Maribel has a fiery presence, igniting
interesting conversations and debates." In speaking of another diverse candidate, a referee noted that "Olivia is easy going and gets along beautifully
with her peers; she is extremely bright and emotionally well-balanced (yet
there's no chip on her shoulder and no hint of 'know it all')."

As noted, the academic literature on references sheds light on a tendency to use "doubt-raising" language in letters for female candidates.
Such language does appear in references for women for leadership-oriented
scholarships: "while Saudi Arabia can be a difficult country for a woman,
Elizabeth still was able to have a good experience." Some problematic language pertained to the applicant's academic performance (keep in mind
that a high grade-point average is not a requirement for some of these
scholarships). One referee observed that a candidate "is a very good student and was very dependable in class. . . . Other students usually looked
to her for help in the class and she helped them as best she could."

The Role of the Advisor

The program directors' consensus that damaging, gender-based commentary occurs only in isolated instances makes it incumbent on campus
scholarship advisors to be vigilant with respect to the language used in letters of reference. Once a letter has been drafted, however, an intervention
may not be possible. Campus advisors do not have access to candidates'
recommendations for every competition, and raising problematic language
with a referee can be a challenging undertaking.

Despite these obstacles, advisors can take steps to promote a culture
of good reference writing on campus. Applicants can be educated about
the role that they play in ensuring the quality of the letters written on
their behalf. Students should know that requesting a recommendation on
short notice or providing insufficient information on the award sought
or the leadership experience to which the referee must attest is not just
bad form; it can result in a testimonial that relies on social stereotypes
rather than providing a detail-rich description of the candidate. A letter

prepared under such challenging circumstances may also lack the context that would help a reader to understand how the student's best qualities connect to measurable leadership outcomes. On some campuses, students receive training and/or tutoring in their first year on how to engage faculty around letters of recommendation and mentoring. For first-generation students especially, this type of training can be helpful for navigating a process that can seem unpredictable and a set of actors who, at times, can seem intimidating and arbitrary.

To guide faculty in writing references for major competitions, American University provides students with a "letter of recommendation request form" to share with the referee. This form explains the selection criteria as our office understands them, including the program's philosophy of leadership. The form also makes clear expectations of the applicant including reference solicitation deadlines and materials to be provided in order to support the referee in the letter-writing process. Students should also understand the etiquette surrounding references, including the importance of notifying the letter writer of the ultimate competition outcome. Additional materials can help campus advisors to raise referees' awareness of the phenomenon of gender stereotyping. The National Center for Women and Information Technology[20] and the University of Arizona Commission on the Status of Women have developed online handouts on how to avoid gender bias in letters of recommendation.[21]

Addressing effective letter writing on an institutional level can be challenging. Referees may feel inundated by the number of recommendation requests they receive each term, and the work they invest in these letters is often invisible to university administrators who decide on merit increases. Under these circumstances, it is difficult to make a case that the letter-writing process for a highly competitive scholarship with multifaceted selection criteria should be an iterative one.

An advisor charged with reviewing letters of recommendation at the campus level faces time management challenges as well. The most detailed letters often arrive at the very end of the application cycle, when the student's proposal is close to its final form and the referee is in a strong position to say what the student is trying to accomplish, why her work matters, and how she is qualified. For advisors, the last few weeks of a competition are frequently a whirlwind of reviewing letters, writing endorsements, and helping students over the finish line. At such times, it is possible to miss subtleties in phrasing that might reflect problems in the characterization of the candidate's leadership.

In contrast, when a candidate receives a scholarship, both the scholar and the advisor have an opportunity and, possibly, the luxury of time in which to frame the achievement for a wider audience, including future referees. Campus press releases and university web pages are indispensable vehicles for raising awareness of a scholarship's criteria and the ways in which the applicant has matched them. Thank-you letters also can remind referees and their supervisors of the criteria by expressing appreciation for the way in which the letter writer has captured a specific aspect of the selection criteria through a description of the candidate.

Although young women dominate the cohorts of scholars selected by leadership-oriented awards, the references written in support of their candidacies do not always contribute to their success. In reviewing recommendations written on behalf of female candidates, scholarship advisors should be aware of gendered language and gender stereotypes that are well documented in the literature on letters of recommendation. This literature focuses on references written for women candidates for faculty and postdoctoral research positions, where scholarly potential is the major criterion; however, it clearly is relevant to other contexts. Although the means at their disposal are not limitless, advisors can take a series of steps to promote a culture of letter writing that addresses such issues on their individual campuses.

Notes

1. Kuheli Dutt et al., "Gender Differences in Recommendation Letters for Postdoctoral Fellowships in Geoscience," *Nature Geoscience* 9 (2016): 805–8.

2. Cf. Frances Trix and Carolyn Psenka, "Exploring the Color of Glass: Letters of Recommendation for Female and Male Medical Faculty," *Discourse & Society* 14, no. 2 (2003): 191–220.

3. Toni Schmader, Jessica Whitehead, and Vicki H. Wysocki, "A Linguistic Comparison of Letters of Recommendation for Male and Female Chemistry and Biochemistry Job Applicants," *Sex Roles* 57, no. 7–8 (2007): 509–14.

4. Dutt et al., "Gender Differences," 805–8.

5. Ibid., 806.

6. Arika Hoffman et al., "Gendered Differences in Letters of Recommendation for Transplant Surgery Fellowship Applicants," *Journal of Surgical Education* 76, no. 2 (2019): 427–432, https://doi.org/10.1016/j.jsurg.2018.08.021.

7. Ibid., 3.

8. Ibid., 3.

9. Juan M. Madera, Michelle R. Hebl, and Randi C. Martin, "Gender and Letters of Recommendation for Academia: Agentic and Communal Differences," *Journal of Applied Psychology* 94, no. 6: 1591–99, http://www.academic.umn.edu/wfc/rec%20letter%20study%202009.pdf.

10. N. Y. Osman et al., "Textual Analysis of Internal Medicine Residency Personal Statements: Themes and Gender Differences," *Medical Education* 49 (2014): 93–102, https://doi-org/10.1111/medu.12487.

11. Virginia Valian, "Beyond Gender Schemas: Improving the Advancement of Women in Academia," *Hypatia* 20, no. 3 (2005): 198–213.

12. Cf. Madera, Hebl, and Randi C. Martin, "Gender and Letters," 1591–99; Juan M. Madera et al., "Raising Doubt in Letters of Recommendation for Academia: Gender Differences and Their Impact," *Journal of Business and Psychology*, https://www.researchgate.net/publication/324782644_Raising_Doubt_in_Letters_of_Recommendation_for_Academia_Gender_Differences_and_Their_Impact; Schmader, Whitehead, and Wysocki, "Linguistic Comparison," 509–14.

13. Madera, Hebl, and Martin, "Gender and Letters," 1591–99.

14. Madera et al., "Raising Doubt in Letters."

15. S. Li et al., "Gender Differences in Language of Standardized Letter of Evaluation Narratives for Emergency Medicine Residency Applicants," *AEM Education and Training* 1, no. 4 (2017): 334–40, https://doi.org/10.1002/aet2.10057.

16. Charles B. Rangel International Affairs Program: https://apply.rangelprogram.org/Default.asp.

17. The Harry S. Truman Scholarship Foundation: https://www.truman.gov/are-you-potential-truman-scholar.

18. Udall Foundation: https://www.udall.gov/ourprograms/ourprograms.aspx.

19. Ibid.

20. National Center for Women and Information Technology, "Promising Practices: Avoiding Unintended Gender Bias in Letters of Recommendation (Case Study 1). Reducing Unconscious Bias to Increase Women's Success in IT," https://www.ncwit.org/sites/default/files/resources/avoidingunintendedgenderbiaslettersrecommendation.pdf.

21. University of Arizona Commission on the Status of Women. "Avoiding Gender Bias in Reference Writing," https://csw.arizona.edu/sites/default/files/avoiding_gender_bias_in_letter_of_reference_writing.pdf.

6

"Well, I arranged the meeting—I arranged the menu, the venue, the seating"

Best Practices for Scholarship Advisors in Managing the Room Where It Happens

DOUG CUTCHINS AND GREG LLACER

Doug Cutchins is director of global awards at New York University Abu Dhabi. He has been an active member of the National Association of Fellowships Advisors (NAFA) since 2001 and has served on the organization's executive board (2005–2009), as its vice-president (2009–2011), and president (2011–2013). Cutchins was the principal organizer of NAFA's 2011 conference in Chicago, and coauthored the 2015 conference proceedings. He has also served as a selection committee member for several national scholarships and fellowships, including the Truman, Udall, Madison, Critical Language, and Dell Foundation Scholarships, and served as a consultant to several colleges, universities, and foundations seeking to improve their advising services. He holds a BA in history from Grinnell College and an MA in history from the University of Connecticut.

Greg A. Llacer is director of the Office of Undergraduate Research and Fellowships at Harvard University and has been a member of NAFA since 2012. In addition to his Harvard responsibilities, Llacer is editorial chair of the national Mellon-Mays Undergraduate Research Journal and director of the Global Program Office for Amgen Scholars, a consortium of twenty-four international undergraduate summer research programs focused on biotechnology. Llacer has served in several key administrative roles, including institutional director of postdoctoral affairs and interim chief of staff for the vice provost of research (in Harvard's Office of the President and Provost), manager of educational initiatives at Harvard-MIT's Division of Health Sciences and Technology, and senior research analyst for the vice chancellor for research at University of San Diego (UCSD). Llacer received an AB degree from San Diego State University in liberal studies with an emphasis on education, and conducted postgraduate study at UCSD and San Diego State University focused on policy studies in language and cross-cultural education.

A mong many of the important responsibilities of a scholarships advisor or fellowships coordinator is defining and administering the process to select applicants for endorsement or, in the case of institutional honors, to receive awards. The process should consider all of the variables that are specific to the award, which in most cases will require a system for vetting candidates that includes some kind of independent and/or committee review by administrator or faculty readers. The purpose of this paper is to provide a guiding framework that could be applied, in whole or in part, to the full range of NAFA institutional profiles.

PART I: Before the Meeting

WHAT ARE THE PROGRAM NEEDS? WHAT SELECTION FORMAT SHOULD BE CONSIDERED?

Before contemplating the process, scholarship advisors should be fully aware of program goals and guidelines. Regardless of how the process is ultimately defined and launched, applicants will likely ask many questions.

The degree to which the scholarships advisor understands the program parameters also will be valuable to a committee of selectors, especially during the deliberation process. Perhaps obvious, the process should start with what the program is seeking, and move backward from there. For instance, if ultimately the goal is to identify four candidates to endorse, depending on the number of applications submitted, it may make sense to develop a two-tier system: first an independent read among the reviewers using a rating system and criteria reference or rubric, then a meeting during which "finalists" are considered and final decisions are made. However, in dealing with only a few candidates, a more streamlined process may be employed: the selectors could be asked for independent reviews and ratings, calculate the outcome (or rankings), and then determine whether or not a meeting is necessary. If the scores are rated and ranked similarly, simply notifying the selectors and suggesting the final outcome without having to meet in person could be more efficient. If there is a fair degree of variance, however, a conversation among committee members will be useful, if not necessary. Unless a specific process is required by faculty governance, or some other administrative rules at your institution, it will ultimately be up to the scholarships advisor or the designated chair to blaze the path for the selectors.

WHO SHOULD THE SELECTORS BE? HOW MANY SHOULD BE CHOSEN?

The identified program parameters will be the first step in considering the makeup of a selection committee. The description of the fellowship or scholarship certainly will contain clues about who might make an insightful reviewer. Thoughtfully pondering provided guidelines as the profile of the selection panel is defined will be invaluable; answering key questions will be essential:

- Are there specific disciplinary requirements?
- Are there faculty who already are familiar with (or have received) the award?
- Are there individuals who have a strong affinity for undergraduates?
- Is the full possible range of variables that contribute to the diversity of a panel (e.g., personal demographics and comportment, length of tenure, etc.) being considered?

- What faculty can look past the interests of their own departments when selecting top candidates?
- Should committee members outside the faculty be considered?
- Among potential selectors, would someone make a good chair, or will someone else, such as the scholarship-advisor, serve in that capacity?

Panel composition depends on established processes and the degree to which institutional senior leadership wants or requires breadth in the decision making. A greater number of panelists may be in order if a deeper vetting process is desired; a very small group may make less contentious judgments. Again, the chosen path is largely dependent on an analysis of what would be appropriate for the specific program as well as the particular institution, leading to outcomes that will bear scrutiny and have veracity among the full range of your constituents. Whatever the size and composition of the committee of selectors, an odd number, no fewer than three, is recommended, to avoid even splits among committee members if a deliberation stalls without a summary decision. If, for instance, the panel is made up of four individuals and there is an unbreakable tie, will the scholarships advisor be the one to break it? Should the scholarship advisor want that responsibility, and is it appropriate having possibly worked with the candidates beforehand?

Whether a faculty chair is necessary (and who it will be), or if the scholarship advisor will be steering, the process needs to be established prior to inviting the entire group to participate. In many instances, depending on how involved or informed senior administrators are, having a faculty chair lends scholarly credibility to the process, as opposed to an administrative or transactional one. In some cases, however, faculty may be reluctant to steer or engage other faculty in this role. A possible middle ground could be identifying a chair and coordinating with that person as a collaborator before a meeting so the roles and the intended goals of the meeting are clearly defined.

HOW SHOULD THE CALENDAR BE SET?

Unfortunately, in any process with a deadline, time rarely is an ally. That is especially true when relying on faculty availability to make decisions. As with determining the selection process more broadly, working from the deadline backward to determine how to set the calendar should provide the necessary time span in the calendar to be effective and comprehensive. Some questions to consider include:

- How much time is necessary for the selection committee to review applications?
- In an endorsement process, will the candidates need time following notification to complete or revise their dossiers?
- Is there another process entirely that follows selection, such as composing institutional endorsement letters?

In all cases, budgeting time as generously as possible is ideal. In those instances, with deadlines that come at the beginning of the academic year, strategically consider the feasibility of setting up a system for applicants to submit and possibly engage the selection committee before the academic term even begins.

WHAT TO SAY IN THE INVITE?

When contacting faculty to participate, it is important to remember to provide as much information as possible, to be concise with instructions, to be flexible when scheduling meetings, and to build in an opportunity for them to politely say no if they need to do so.

In general, sharing with the dean or provost that overtures are being made to faculty for service and getting their validation is a good idea. If, for instance, an invitation begins with "On behalf of Dean X and Provost Y," the recipient will be more likely to pay attention and keep reading. Following a brief introductory statement inviting them to serve on a committee, the advisor should provide an equally brief synopsis of the award and the charge of the committee. Then, follow up with an overall timetable for the scholarship process—application deadline, when committee members should expect dossiers, when they should return ratings (if applicable), and potential meeting dates. Finally, they should be thanked for considering the appointment and encouraged to respond at their earliest convenience.

Keep the invitation short—three paragraphs tops, and be prepared to resend. Copy a faculty's staff assistant (if there is one) on the original message to increase the chances that the faculty member will respond or that the timeline will make the calendar.

HOW DOES THE SCHOLARSHIP ADVISOR SELECT THE LOCALE?

Depending on space availability at the institution, setting the location of the meeting may matter to the faculty selected to be on the committee. More often than not, faculty respond positively when they are accommodated to the extent possible when it comes to travel from their own offices, especially on large campuses. So, choosing the path and environment of least resistance is prudent. Select a comfortably sized conference room that is as equidistant among the selectors as is feasible. Once a good space has been identified, knowing how the room is configured is essential: Will a whiteboard (or LCD projector and screen) be needed to organize the names of finalists for comparison? Is the table configured for robust conversation? Will the conversation be truly confidential? What other variables are there (ventilation, windows/glare, lighting) that could contribute to the quality of the experience and likelihood that a faculty member will sign on again at a future date?

WHAT SHOULD BE PROVIDED BEFORE THE MEETING?

Once the panel is set, a negotiation among the committee members for the timing of the actual meeting (if there is going to be one) may have to be coordinated, within the general time expressed in the invitation. Each committee member should be canvassed independently and then all addressed in a subsequent email with the actual date, time, and location.

This confirmation may also be used to find out whether the members of the committee would prefer their materials electronically or on paper. Although most faculty now prefer receiving applications as pdf files, some still request paper, or both. Being as flexible as possible will win friends among faculty. If necessary, the paper package should be hand delivered to the office of the reviewer. If there is information about candidates on the application that is FERPA protected, such as birthdate or ethnicity, only the encrypted form of file transfer protocol required for transmission by the institution should be used.

Now that all of the logistical details are set, the committee members should be sent a single package that includes all of the information necessary to independently evaluate the candidates, including the following:

- Description of the scholarship or fellowship award from the source
- Any FAQs from the source that may be helpful for the reviewers to use

- A criteria reference/rubric to rate the applicants (more on that below) and instructions for ratings
- A blank tally sheet to record the ratings
- The applications assigned to the reviewer
- A cover letter explaining the process (e.g., independent review followed by a committee meeting—whether optional, required, or if necessary); for electronic delivery, this "letter" could be the introductory email

Depending on the number of applications, it may be helpful to determine whether or not the committee needs *all* of the documentation. If the decisions could be made with a more streamlined approach, then doing so would make for happier reviewers. For instance, the Rhodes Scholarship includes a relatively large number of recommendations, but does the committee need every letter to make an endorsement decision? If not, how many provide enough information without overwhelming the committee members?

Emphasizing the due date for the recipient of the ratings is important (if by email, copy the individual, or if by campus mail, include a return envelope). Also highlight the date, time, and location of the meeting (if there will be one), even if the meeting has already been sent to their campus calendars. The intention is for the faculty reviewers to work as efficiently as possible—when using electronic files, everything should be labeled clearly and consistently. If using paper files, the order of documents needs to be the same as what is described in the cover message.

WHAT ABOUT PRE-MEETING RATINGS AND INSTRUCTIONS?

The materials sent (including the rubric) to the selectors for their independent review should make the evaluation process clear. Some (but not all!) of the possibilities include the following:

- A short list of priority candidates
- A top-to-bottom ranking of candidates
- A three-point Likert rating scale (YES, MAYBE, NO)
- A three-point Likert rating scale with the ability to use decimal numbers
- A five-point Likert rating scale

Of the three Likert scale choices, the ability to use decimal numbers on a three-point scale is probably the most effective, if only for the reason that the criteria reference will have three major emphases: a strong candidate, a moderately qualified candidate, and a less qualified candidate. Of course, this can be done with a five-point scale as well, but there likely will be more stratification of numbers among committee members, making final decisions more difficult. A three-point scale compresses the numbers and encourages the reviewers to make stark choices. It is also important to point out that within a criteria reference, there likely will be three or four points to assess, some of which are strong, others not so much. The rubric should be specific for each of the major scaling ratings, and address all of the descriptive criteria (and possibly eligibility criteria) with differentiation among those ratings to discern what highly qualified, moderately qualified, and marginally qualified (or unqualified) candidates look like.

Consider again, for instance, the Marshall Scholarship, for which the broad criteria include academic success, leadership experience, and evidence of a connection to the United Kingdom through and beyond the term of the fellowship. A fifth "bullet" could be strength of the writing sample, if indeed the process includes an opportunity for the committee to review a statement of intent.

If using a three- or five-point Likert scale, then it is very likely that many candidates will demonstrate strength in some of the criteria but not necessarily all. As a preamble to the criteria, it is a good idea to briefly explain this, and that scores between integers (i.e., 1.25, 2.5, or whatever scale works best for the office) are okay. Making clear what the high score is—whether it be the lowest possible number (1 on a 1–3 scale) or the highest number (3 on a 1–3 scale)—will save confusion later as some faculty will have a preconceived notion of what they consider "high" and "low" in a numeric scale.

The final point to the committee should be to look out for unintended bias as they give their ratings (see Paula Warrick's article on gender bias in letters of recommendation in this volume). Some may be so influenced by one indicator in the criteria that they disregard all others, leaving a rating that does not reflect all of the variables as described in the award (and hopefully the criteria reference). Even if a gentle warning is included in the instructions, it still may be that you have disagreements among panelists in the ratings, which will have to be sorted out through a nuanced calculation process and the meeting (if there is one).

PART II: The Meeting

Once all the work of setting up a committee meeting is done, the scholarship advisor then must run the meeting itself and lead the committee to the conclusion of candidate nomination or selection. Even if a scholarship advisor has followed all of the available best practices in organizing the meeting, leading and administering the meeting itself requires a different skill set and provides a new list of challenges and opportunities. Running an effective, efficient, and successful meeting can be demanding, but it is a necessary skill to develop in order to reach successful outcomes for applicants.

WHAT IS THE MINDSET OF COMMITTEE MEMBERS WALKING INTO A SCHOLARSHIP NOMINATION OR AWARD MEETING?

While the committee meetings that scholarship advisors run is, of course, central to the work advisors do, and essential to their success, this is not necessarily true for the faculty, staff, and community members who populate these committees. While serving on a selection panel can be a deeply interesting, intellectually engaging, and professionally rewarding experience, committee members are also usually busy people who are volunteering to add this role on to the rest of their busy job and life outside of work. Yes, they may find some enthusiasm for serving on this committee, but they may also have an already-full plate of research, writing, advising, teaching, editing, reviewing, and being administrators. A central principle to remember in running these meetings is that while the committee members have volunteered to help and want to do a good job, they also want the work to be as pleasurable, interesting, and straightforward as possible. Therefore, it is incumbent on scholarship advisors to honor the committee members' time by holding meetings that are well administered, focus on the task at hand, and display respect for the committee members' dedication.

HOW CAN SCHOLARSHIP ADVISORS START THE MEETING OUT ON A POSITIVE NOTE?

In order to capitalize on the goodwill of committee members and to minimize the recalcitrance some may feel walking into the meeting room, scholarship advisors need to begin meetings with as positive, upbeat, and welcoming a tone as possible. Remember that many of these meetings happen at times of day and during moments of the academic year when committee members may already be stressed and overworked and that they are often walking into this meeting as a volunteer. While they may have agreed to participate on the committee with enthusiasm, and while there may be some part of them that is looking forward to the conversation with other committee members or interviews with candidates, it is also possible that this can become just one more task to accomplish in a long day.

One reliable, easy, and low-budget way to help start any meeting on a positive note is to provide food and beverages. While it is nice if the scholarship advisor can provide relatively substantive fare, especially for meetings that happen over mealtimes, refreshments do not have to be extravagant or expensive: fruit skewers, cookies and crackers, and tea or water will usually suffice. Providing provisions to committee members sends a clear message of appreciation for their work, gives them caloric intake for the energy that they will expend during the meeting, and can create a convivial atmosphere from the start in which the group feels like it is working together toward a common goal. Feeding committee members may be the best, most effective way to create a positive atmosphere in a meeting.

Scholarship advisors should arrive well before the meeting start time to make sure that the room is indeed clear for the committee meeting, check any technology that will be used to connect to interviewees or committee members in other places, clear any remnants of previous meetings, set up the table and chairs in the ideal configuration, ensure that the refreshments have arrived and are in the correct location, and calm the nerves of any early-arriving interviewees. Arriving early also gives the scholarship advisor the opportunity to greet committee members as they arrive, assure them that they have found the right room, and answer any individualized questions that a committee member may have before others arrive. Overall, arriving early allows scholarship advisors to set a positive tone for the committee members by demonstrating competence, efficiency, and gratitude for faculty participation.

WHAT SHOULD THE SCHOLARSHIP ADVISOR BRING TO THE MEETING?

While scholarship advisors can rely on most committee members to come fully prepared for the meeting, it is always a good idea to have backups in case someone is unprepared, a laptop dies at an inopportune moment, or a committee member forgets a file. Having one or two hard copies of all of the application materials, which can be passed to a committee member who needs them, can be helpful, though this may not always be plausible if the materials run into hundreds of pages. If the committee will be conducting interviews, consider bringing a hard copy of the interview schedule to the meeting, so that each committee member is aware of the order of interviews; this can also serve as a visual reminder to members to move things along if the committee is running behind schedule as the meeting progresses. The scholarship advisor should also bring loose-leaf paper and extra pens for committee members who wish to take handwritten notes but who forget to bring the necessary supplies. Paper and pens can also be handy for confidential voting or opinion polling later in the meeting.

HOW SHOULD THE ROOM BE SET UP FOR THE MEETING?

While how a room is set up may seem like a pedantic detail, the scholarship advisor should keep in mind how the configuration may best support the process. If using a whiteboard or LCD projector to record the decision-making process during deliberations (e.g., listing or grouping names), then make sure that everyone on the committee can see without twisting or turning awkwardly. In particular, if using an LCD projector, test the format before the committee arrives. For instance, if using MS-Excel to illuminate candidate comparisons, make sure the text on the screen is not too small to read—however, if enlarged, the number of columns or cells may be reduced. Knowing this in advance will allow the advisor to solve the problem without the stress of committee members watching. At the very least, the room setup should allow for easy conversation and collaboration; even where individuals sit around a table should be thoughtfully considered.

WHAT SHOULD THE SCHOLARSHIP ADVISOR SAY IN THE CHARGE TO THE COMMITTEE AT THE START OF THE MEETING?

The meeting usually will begin with the scholarship advisor speaking at some length to set the tone and expectations for it. Even if the scholarship advisor is not serving as the committee chair, the advisor will usually start the meeting with a few words before handing it off to the chair for further instructions. This opening preamble should be planned in advance in order to coalesce all of the committee members around an agreed purpose for the meeting, make clear what the outcome of the meeting should be, and set a welcoming, collegial tone. To that end, some of the first words out of the scholarship advisor's mouth should be "Thank you." Even if the committee has been thanked multiple times via email for serving, expressing gratitude in person is not only polite, but also makes clear to the committee members how appreciated their service is, making them more likely to continue to approach the work positively.

The opening instructions for the committee often take ten to fifteen minutes to deliver and should include some or all of the following elements:

- Meeting logistics, including the location of restrooms and a clear indication if the committee will be taking a break at some point or if committee members should excuse themselves if need be.
- A brief review of the award being considered, including key selection criteria. This can be particularly important later in the meeting if committee members start bringing their own criteria or desires to the discussion, outside the stated, official award criteria.
- An overview of the meeting's agenda, especially if interviews are involved, and an indication of what time the scholarship advisor hopes the meeting will conclude, which gives everyone a goal and helps keep the committee focused on finishing in a timely way.
- If interviewing, the kinds of questions that should be asked and guidelines on how aggressive or collegial the tone of the questions should be.
- If interviewing, guidance on how the interview will progress: should committee members have the same questions for each candidate or different questions for each candidate? Will one person ask the same opening warm-up question of each candidate? If so, who is asking that question and what will it be? Will the committee take turns asking questions, or should individuals jump in as they have questions?
- An indication of how decisions will be made at the end of the conversation. This is particularly important if the committee will be asked to vote or rank candidates at the end of interviews or the conversation, as is often helpful. Committee members also need

to know in advance if they should be holding a mental ranking of candidates as the meeting progresses.

- An invitation for those who have served on the committee in the past to speak briefly about what best practices they bring with them from their previous work. Returning committee members often have one piece of advice, a framing device, or simply words of encouragement for the other committee members that come with an authority and genuineness that the rest of the group appreciates.
- A few moments for committee members to ask questions and feel clear on the award, criteria, and process for interviews, decision making, and meeting outcomes.

Finally, the scholarship advisor can promote collegiality and consensus by encouraging committee members to do three things during the meeting:

1. *Speak their minds.* Silent committee members are not helpful to the process; they are there to help make a decision, which requires speaking up about the candidates. Encourage committee members to own and defend their beliefs about the applicants.

2. *Respect one another's opinions.* At the same time, committee members must recognize that there is almost always disagreement among the people in the room, and that those areas of disagreement are real, intellectually honest, and truly held. All committee members have a right to an opinion; they do not, however, get to claim that they have the best opinion. While committee members need to have and articulate their opinions, they also need to be reminded diplomatically to listen carefully to their colleagues.

3. *Seek consensus.* Committee members should simultaneously seek to persuade other committee members and be open to being persuaded by others. Committee members should resist digging in, but should seek to understand others' opinions and why areas of difference exist. The committee should respectfully work together toward a consensus opinion. Consensus does not mean unanimity, as areas of disagreement may still exist at the end of the meeting. Instead, it indicates that the committee members have reached an outcome that, even if some individuals disagree with it personally, everyone can consent to as the will of the group as a whole.

WHAT IS THE SCHOLARSHIP ADVISOR'S ROLE ONCE THE MEETING STARTS?

The scholarship advisor plays several distinct and important roles in the meeting itself:

- *Keeper of time.* The scholarship advisor needs to keep the meeting moving, remembering that efficient meetings engender goodwill among committee members, which makes them more likely to return in future years or for other committees. This is especially true if the committee's work involves interviews, which must be scheduled carefully in advance, and then adhered to strictly during the meeting. Doing so not only ensures that the committee finishes its work at the time when the advisor promised they would be done, but also gives each candidate equal time in front of the committee. Scholarship advisors need to walk a careful line between encouraging the conversation to move along and not rushing committee members toward an outcome.

- *Enforcer of scholarship criteria.* There are two ways in which the scholarship advisor must enforce a scholarship's stated criteria. First, the advisor must ensure that all criteria are being followed, and that the committee is not ignoring a criterion that is important to the funding agency; if the criteria call for a candidate who has a strong track record of community service, for example, and the committee is not taking that factor into account, the scholarship advisor needs to point this out. Second, the scholarship advisor must ensure that committee members are not inventing criteria that are personally important to them or their work, but that are meaningless to the funding agency. A committee member from the mathematics department who insists that a student cannot be successful on their creative writing Fulbright because they have not had a quantitative reasoning class since their first year, for example, needs to be corrected by the scholarship advisor that this is not a barrier to the student's success in the competition.

- *Seeker of consensus.* The scholarship advisor should pay close attention to the committee members' opinions throughout the meeting, both by listening carefully to their comments and by looking for nonverbal cues of agreement and disagreement.

Committee members may be reticent to point out areas of disagreement, or to name the fact that consensus is building in favor of a particular candidate. Both of these are necessary tasks for the scholarship advisor to undertake in order to help the committee move forward toward a decision. Using phrases such as, "Listening to all of you speak, it strikes me that the following candidates seem to have a lot of support, while the others may not be at that level; do you all agree with that?" will help the committee conclude its work more quickly and harmoniously.

- *Corrector of erroneous information.* Though less likely, it is possible that one or more members of the committee will simply be discussing factual errors about a candidate, such as their major, whether or not they studied abroad, the languages they speak, etc. Scholarship advisors need to have the basic facts of each candidate committed to memory, or at least to have a sense of the students at play, in order to ensure the committee is making decisions based on correct information.
- *Collector of documents to be shredded.* At the conclusion of the meeting, the scholarship advisor should collect all printed documents from committee members, as well as all paper votes or other confidential information, and ensure that they are shredded in order to protect the confidentiality of the applicants and the decision-making process.

Scholarship advisors should not be, by and large, conveyors of personal opinions. The scholarship advisor, in most cases, is the convener and administrator of the meeting but is not a committee member and should not vote or voice an opinion, even in close decisions or in cases of a tie on the committee. The main reason for this is that there are conflicts of interest involved in being both an advisor to students and a decision-maker on the committee. Students need to know that they can trust their scholarship advisor; be open about their hopes, dreams, and hesitations in advising meetings; and not feel like they are sending drafts of documents to someone for advice who will ultimately judge them. Scholarship advisors may be tempted to voice an opinion during a committee meeting, and committee members will often expect or invite scholarship advisors to speak their minds. Resist this temptation. Allow the committee to make the decision, based on the materials and information presented to them. Remember that there is not an objective right or wrong answer for the committee to reach, and they may reach a decision different from the one the scholarship advisor would make. Scholarship advisors must be humble enough and trust their committee members enough to accept outcomes, even those that they do not prefer. In the end, the scholarship advisor's job is to set the committee up to successfully make the best decision it can, regardless of whether or not the scholarship advisor would make the same decision.

HOW SHOULD THE SCHOLARSHIP ADVISOR HELP THE COMMITTEE REACH A DECISION?

As noted above, if the committee is reaching a decision without interviews, polling them in advance of the meeting to understand where they stand as a group can be helpful. Doing so can involve asking them to rate candidates on a Likert scale, or to send a short list of their top candidates, or to rank the candidates from top to bottom. In general, it is a great time-saver if committee members have voiced their individual opinions before arriving in the meeting room, which gives everyone a chance both to be heard equally and to allow for the beginning of a consensus opinion to be reached.

If the committee's work includes interviewing candidates, the scholarship advisor may want to ask the committee to wait to discuss individual candidates and any coming decisions until all interviews are completed. If not, committees may be tempted to make decisions before all interviews have finished, perhaps giving early interviewees an unfair advantage or disadvantage; what seems like a particularly strong or weak candidate early on in the evening may be perceived differently by comparison after all interviews have finished. Once all interviews have finished, the scholarship advisor should begin the deliberative stage of the meeting by polling the committee individually, much as would have been done before the meeting began if there were not interviews. This polling should be done individually and privately so that each committee member can voice their opinions about the candidates without outside influence from the other committee members; this ensures that no one committee member has an outsized voice at the start.

Once the committee members have all had a chance to make their voices heard, either through pre-meeting or post-interview polling, the scholarship advisor should examine the result of the poll and frame the conversation for the committee. The initial polls should generally not be used as a decision-making tool, since the committee will usually want to discuss the candidates. There may be, for example, one committee member who has a different opinion from the rest after reading the files, and who can make a persuasive argument in person. It is common for one or two candidates to be nearly universally praised by the committee, a number to be judged as noncompetitive, and a swath of candidates to be assigned to the midrange for additional discussion. Scholarship advisors may also use pre-meeting or post-interview rating tools to suss out which candidates will take the most conversation, or to discover where gulfs of difference in opinion exist on the committee. If one committee member has a student highly ranked and another committee member has that same student ranked quite low, it is helpful for the scholarship advisor to figure this out and to raise this issue early on in the meeting.

For the most part, scholarship advisors should attempt to help the committee reach a consensus decision through targeted questions. Examples of such questions include:

- Asking committee members to briefly discuss each candidate about whom a consensus opinion does not already exist. In doing so, it is helpful to keep a positive tone by having the committee member who is most enthusiastic about a candidate start the conversation.
- Asking the committee to look back over the selection criteria and speak to the relative strengths and weaknesses of each candidate accordingly.
- Summarizing where the committee is in its deliberations at that moment, and asking what the most difficult questions are facing the committee at that time.
- Asking open-ended questions like "What's on your mind that you have not yet had a chance to say?"

In general, committees will, with the scholarship advisor's help and guidance, find their way to a consensus decision. Committee members may sometimes find themselves at a point where discussion seems to have halted or the group seems to be spinning its wheels, just repeating the same points. At these times, the scholarship advisor may decide to poll the group again, either formally or informally, and either privately via secret ballot or via voice vote, to judge where the committee is in terms of reaching agreement. Doing so can help one or two committee members see that the rest of the members hold contrary opinions, or it can reveal to the group that the room is more united than previously thought.

WHAT SHOULD THE SCHOLARSHIP ADVISOR DO IF THE COMMITTEE IS STUCK AND CANNOT MAKE A CONSENSUS DECISION THROUGH CONVERSATION ALONE?

One of the great advantages of working with committees that are solely or primarily made up of academics is that they generally value one another's opinions, are open to being swayed by superior arguments, and value intellectual honesty in decision making. Most committees will be able to reach a consensus decision through discussion of the candidates, and do not need to resort to further means to reach a final outcome.

When committees are truly stuck, there are a few methods scholarship advisors can use to move the committee forward:

- Determine that there really is a split in the numbers and not just a vocal minority of committee members who are being loud in their opinions. Poll the committee members and share the outcomes of that poll with the committee; indicate that there seems to be more support behind one candidate than another.
- Ask one committee member who is particularly vocal in support for a specific candidate to summarize the case for that student, and see if anyone who originally supported a different student is swayed.
- Allow for weighted voting: give each committee member ten points, and allow them to distribute those points among the remaining candidates, with the caveat that they cannot give two candidates the same number of points. This allows committee members who are more enthusiastic about a particular candidate to express themselves. This method requires that committee members approach the task with rigorous intellectual honesty.
- In rare cases, it may be helpful to dismiss the committee without making a decision, and to resume the conversation later. This is

generally inadvisable since subsequent actions in the nomination or award process may be timed to the committee's meeting, and getting the committee back together on a short timeline may be quite difficult. Additionally, the committee may have to make final decisions via email, and not all committee members may be timely with their email responses. Still, in certain situations, a scholarship advisor may decide that the committee will have an easier time reaching a decision if everyone has twenty-four hours to think about their positions and the candidates, or if certain personalities are not present in a room together.

One final point is to continue to keep the clock in mind throughout the decision-making process, and to push the committee toward making a decision as efficiently as possible. Committee members may simply be unhappy about the group not selecting a student that they really liked and wanted to support. They may unconsciously drag out a decision-making process because they feel, at some level, that taking a longer time to finish demonstrates the degree to which they supported a student. Remember that students do not know how long the committee took to make a decision, and that even if they did know, that information is secondary to the main point: they were not chosen.

HOW CAN SCHOLARSHIP ADVISORS AVOID OR MANAGE CONFLICT, PROMOTE COLLEGIALITY, AND HANDLE DIFFICULT PERSONALITIES ON A COMMITTEE?

Happily, most scholarship committee members are collegial, work toward consensus, and trust their colleagues. In the vast majority of committee meetings, scholarship advisors will find that the committee members work together efficiently, listen to one another, and are willing both to argue with and be swayed by others' arguments. Sometimes, however, one or more committee members will act outside of this established norm, which can be a significant challenge for the scholarship advisor. Here are a few best practices in avoiding and managing difficult personalities on a scholarship committee:

- Bringing together a committee of people who know one another already, or who know that they may be working together in the future, can be enormously useful. In this sense, having some committee members who know that they will be returning for future years on the same committee can inspire them to work collegially in two ways. First, they know that they will be sitting around this table again, giving them an incentive to make this a positive experience. Second, committee members may feel that establishing a trusting relationship with one another may lead to future give-and-take: "if I give in to your argument this year, which I may not be as invested in, it is more likely that you may give in to my argument next year, which I may be more invested in."

- The scholarship advisor's preamble, discussed above, is crucial in setting the tone for the meeting. The idea of having everyone speak, listen, and seek consensus is absolutely necessary for the success of the meeting. If scholarship advisors can get everyone to buy into that idea from the start, they can later gently return to that notion if one or more committee members are not cooperating appropriately.

- Having a trusted committee member who is a senior member of the faculty, who has served on this committee in the past, who held this scholarship themselves, or who has some other voice of authority in the decision-making process can be an asset to the scholarship advisor. With such perceived authority, this figure can help manage difficult personalities on the committee by helping to note past practices or examples of how the committee has made decisions previously.

- If necessary, the scholarship advisor can poll the group and point out to a holdout that they are alone (or nearly alone) in their opinion. While this may not convince everyone to seek consensus, it helps both that individual and the rest of the room understand the situation at hand. Using phrases like "In the interest of time . . ." or "In order to help us move this meeting toward a final decision . . ." may help remind the room of the task at hand and the necessity of wrapping up the committee's work.

- Finally, scholarship advisors should make note of which committee members did their jobs well and to be sure to invite them back. Keeping notes on which committee members prepared in advance by reading application and foundation materials, arrived on time, came ready to participate, spoke and owned their opinions, listened to their colleagues, and sought consensus will help advisors develop committees that work together seamlessly. Similarly, advisors should note committee members who did not do one or more of those things. Those in the first group should be reinvited for many years to come; those in the latter group are best avoided in future years.

PART III: Post-meeting Responsibilities

Once the scholarship committee meeting has concluded, the committee's work is done for the most part. The scholarship advisor will then launch into the next stages of the process, including notifying students of outcomes, working with nominees for national awards on the submission process, etc. While committee members may not have a formal role in the rest of the process, the scholarship advisor does need to follow up with the committee in two important ways post-meeting.

The first is simply to express gratitude once again for their participation in the meeting. This does not necessarily need to be an extensive thanks, especially since many faculty members see participating in such committees as part of the job. In most cases, a short email of thanks, sent to the entire committee the following morning, will suffice. On some campuses, or in specific cases such as with an untenured junior faculty member, it may make sense for the scholarship advisor to send a more formal written thank-you letter, perhaps copying in the faculty member's department chair, dean, or even the provost. Some universities invite committee members to an end-of-year recognition event, such as a reception or dinner, where students who applied for or were nominated for awards are the center of attention, but committee members can also be recognized. If the scholarship advisor's budget has some extra funds at the end of the fiscal year, providing committee members with a small token of gratitude might be possible.

Second, at the conclusion of the meeting and immediately following, it is critical to make sure that the outcome is recorded properly for institutional archives. Before departure, recap the final results with the committee and record them separately in order to refer to the decisions in real-time during the meeting, with the recap at the end as the formal document containing the outcomes, then compare the two to make sure there are no anomalies or misunderstandings about results before informing applicants (or anyone else). Additionally, it is important to know and understand how decision data are collected and kept at the institution, especially if an applicant makes a request for information about scholarship selection processes. If the committee has brought paper copies along to the meeting, collect them and their notes for shredding to make sure that otherwise confidential information documented informally during the process or notes are not accidentally left in the room or in a waste receptacle. The best course of action is to shred all documents except originals that are required to record the deliberations and outcomes.

Finally, advisors will want to keep committee members in the loop as the process continues post-meeting. If the committee met to nominate students for a national award, be sure to let the committee know if the selected students advance as finalists, are selected for interview, and especially if they win. Committee members are invested in the process and outcomes, and would much rather hear the good news from the advisor than from a campus press release. Similarly, if a student sends the scholarship advisor a note that says something to the effect of "I did not win but learned a lot from this process," consider forwarding that to the committee (with the student's permission) so that members can see that outcomes go beyond winning and losing. Honor the committee members' work, effort, and time by keeping them informed of what happens to the students and their applications after the meeting has finished.

Conclusion

The purpose of this paper has been to provide a general, chronological tool for the engagement of faculty in the institutional selection process for applicants or endorsement candidates for internal and external scholarship and fellowship awards. The scholarship advisor's responsibilities are, for the most part, to organize the selection process and to be an expert of content knowledge and institutional context. The committee's role is to weigh the criteria of awards, distinguish the characteristics of candidates, and arrive at conclusions about the ultimate selection. The goal is for the process to be standardized, reasonable, and logical in a way that will yield outcomes that are based on a deep reflection of an established, well-articulated criteria, with veracity and legitimacy, yet with enough flexibility to adjust for institutional priorities and programmatic variations when necessary. Through thoughtful planning and implementation, the scholarship advisor can be an effective strategist in getting faculty reviewers to consensus, designing an exercise that can be stimulating, inspiring, and satisfying.

7

Strategic Planning for Fellowships Offices
Minimizing Challenges, Identifying Stakeholders, and Optimizing Benefits

DACIA CHARLESWORTH

Dacia Charlesworth has served as Butler University's director of undergraduate research and prestigious scholarships since August 2015. From 2012 to 2015, she was a university ambassador for Valdosta State University (VSU); advisor for VSU's chapter of Black Student Journalists; and consultant for the American Institutes of Research, writing test questions for a high-stakes postgraduate entrance examination. From 2008 to 2012, Charlesworth was associate professor of communication and a member of the graduate faculty at Indiana University–Purdue University, Fort Wayne. She served as director of the University Honors Programs (2004–2008) and associate (2004–2008) and assistant professor (2002–2004) of communication at Robert Morris University in Pennsylvania. She also was founding director of the Oral Communication Across the Curriculum Program at Southeast Missouri State University. Charlesworth earned a PhD (2001) and MS (1995) in speech communication from Southern Illinois

University, Carbondale, and a BA in communication from Arizona State University (1994).

When I was hired as Butler University's director of undergraduate research and prestigious scholarships, I felt very comfortable with my knowledge of undergraduate research; however, my work with fellowships and scholarships was limited only to the brief exposure I gained as the director of the University Honors Programs (UHP) at Robert Morris University (RMU). In 2007, RMU's president felt that we needed to begin recruiting for prestigious awards; the provost felt that it made sense that the recruitment of these awards be housed in the UHP. Since I was directing the International Honors Program, the Cooperative Education Honors Program, the International Cooperative Education Honors Program, the Pre-Law Program, and teaching two courses each semester, all I could really do to fulfill the president's request was identify a few select opportunities, add a page to the UHP website with some links to those opportunities, and identify potential applicants within the UHP. In 2008, I left RMU to return to full-time teaching and did not consider prestigious fellowships/scholarships again until I began my current position at Butler University in September 2015.

I was fortunate to attend the National Association of Fellowships Advisors (NAFA) conference in July 2015 prior to beginning my new position. The New Advisors Workshop was invaluable as it provided me with a clear understanding of the types of awards available, their selection criteria, and strategies for submitting competitive applications as well as an overview of advising best practices. After I returned from the conference, I began drafting a concrete plan for beginning a new position on a new campus. Fortunately, I had the entire month of August to reflect on how I would begin my work at Butler.

My reflections took me back to the focus of my first professional position: outcomes assessment. I was hired to develop, implement, and assess an Oral Communication Across the Curriculum program at Southeast Missouri State University in 1998. This position taught me quickly that assessment—done correctly—is a crucial task that ultimately secures departmental autonomy since individual faculty and staff members and departments and other units develop their own outcomes and operationalize what constitutes mastery of those outcomes. Outcome assessment also offers a clear pathway to success that includes observable and measurable indicators from several contexts.

As I thought about my new position and how I would navigate a new campus at Butler, I began considering possible steps to take that would help me to be an effective fellowships advisor. Only after I had written all my ideas on the notepad did I notice how closely aligned my items on the paper were with the strategic planning process. Given my extensive experience with strategic planning at the university, college, and departmental levels, this observation delighted me. Developing a strategic plan for fellowships advising would not only allow me to become familiar with Butler's mission, campus culture, and faculty, but it would also assist me in developing measurable outcomes related to the advising process. My strategic planning process was atypical since I worked on my own and included informal feedback I received during my campus interview and my first few weeks on the job. I supplemented my observations with traditional sources, such as information about the university from its website and accreditation reports.

After realizing the benefits of completing a strategic plan, I wanted to share portions of the strategic planning process that proved to be especially helpful for me as a new fellowships advisor with others. I am certainly not the only fellowships advisor utilizing the strategic planning process. NAFA's 2017 *Survey of the Profession* indicates that of the 20 percent of NAFA members who completed the survey, 59.8 percent reported having strategic goals for their fellowship activities, and 67.4 percent reported engaging in programmatic review; however, only 19.6 percent reported having learning and development outcomes.[1] In addition, 20.7 percent of respondents indicated they plan to develop strategic goals, and 26.8 percent reported plans to create learning and development outcomes.[2] The purpose of this chapter, then, is to provide meaningful information about the strategic planning process for those planning to engage in the process and for those who have strategic goals, but have not yet linked them to specific outcomes. First, an overview of strategic planning is offered. Second, benefits and challenges related to strategic planning are highlighted, followed by the components of strategic planning. Finally, specific materials for identifying, categorizing, and engaging stakeholders are provided.

Strategic Planning Overview

At the heart of the strategic planning process is the desire to ensure a unit is performing at its best, the belief that all future planning must be intentional, and the acknowledgment that this is a continuous process. While there are many definitions of strategic planning, Bryson's definition is one of the most succinct: Strategic planning is a "deliberative, disciplined approach to producing fundamental decisions and actions that shape and guide what an organization is, what it does, and why."[3] Bryson also notes that those engaging in strategic planning must consider the context in which their organization functions; the purposes, goals, and situational requirements of their organization; the strengths, opportunities, weaknesses, and threats of their organization [a SWOT assessment, see pages 176–78 for further discussion]; and the fact that "strategies are both deliberately set in advance and emergent in practice."[4]

The strategic planning process traditionally operates at the highest levels of the organization. One of the first steps in strategic planning is for divisional staff or departmental faculty to clarify their roles and goals within the organization and identify how their roles and goals mesh with the overarching mission and vision of the organization. This information is then shared with division chairpersons, deans, vice presidents, and the president—those intimately familiar with the organization at a "big-picture" level—so that they can reference this information as they carve out a path to move forward. While some fellowships advisors may be part of this larger process, most are likely asked to provide a synthesis of our unit's mission, goals, and the activities we undertake to achieve those goals to our supervisors, who will then incorporate our information in their reports that are ultimately reviewed by the organizational decision makers. If fellowships advisors' organizations do not require them to participate in strategic planning, they should still engage in the strategic planning process themselves to benefit their unit. Those who have completed the strategic planning process are at a distinct advantage when it is time for the organization to be reaccredited, as the plan will demonstrate how the unit operates to fulfill the organization's vision and mission on a variety of levels.

For purposes of clarification, strategic planning is the last step in a larger process and usually occurs once a unit has been reviewed (often

Figure 7.1. Cycle of Strategic Planning Process[6]

referred to as programmatic review). The programmatic review process includes creating or refining the unit's mission, vision, and assessment plan.[5] A programmatic review evaluates an entire unit and its programs as they relate to the organization as a whole, whereas assessment plans measure a unit's accomplishments and students' knowledge, behaviors, and attitudes. While assessment plans are a major component of programmatic reviews, other areas of the review include the unit's centrality to the organization's mission, faculty and staff qualifications and productivity, assessment of the unit's offerings, analysis of the unit's facilities, and synthesis of a unit's access to and use of technology. Essential steps from the programmatic review process and elements of assessment plans are included in this discussion so that no additional reading is required before beginning the strategic planning process. An overview of the cycle is presented in Figure 7.1.

Strategic Planning Benefits and Challenges

Before the strategic planning process can begin, a review of the unit must occur to gain a holistic representation of the unit, those working within the unit, and the unit's operations. By its very nature, the word *review* can instill a sense of apprehension even in those who are exceedingly confident of their unit's worth. The etymology of *review* can be traced back to the Middle French word *revue*, which means to reconsider some subject or thing, and was used as early as 1356 to refer to an inspection of military forces.[7] A cursory consideration of terminology associated with strategic planning reveals its militaristic history (e.g., strategy, competitive advantages, large-scale operation) and affirms the risks embedded in the strategic planning process, such as creating a sound plan based on contextual evidence that could highlight a unit's shortcomings and failures. The process, however, should help an organization to succeed by allowing it to become strategically agile, and transform itself—correcting for flaws in the initial plan—based on changes in the environment and continuous assessment.[8]

For most fellowships advisors, the task of reviewing our units or programs within those units seems daunting. Strategic planning, while a demanding process, has many benefits that ultimately serve to improve the unit. Some of the many benefits include the possibility of creating new positions, adapting unit protocol to be more efficient, being awarded additional office space, and planning strategically for the coming years. Even a primary challenge of strategic planning—identifying the unit's weaknesses or possibly discovering that the unit is not aligned with the organization's mission or vision—has the potential to produce benefits. The positive side of highlighting these weaknesses is the opportunity to discuss the unit's needs and related budget issues with decision makers.

Participating in the strategic planning process may also benefit all members of the unit. Sergiovanni identifies three primary individual benefits:

1. *Ensuring quality control*, as this type of review verifies the unit's goals are consistent with the organization's mission and values
2. *Aiding in participants' professional development*, as this type of review allows individuals involved in the process to grow personally and professionally by continually expanding and enhancing their knowledge, especially as it relates to fellowships advising
3. *Motivating individuals involved by linking them to the success of the unit*, as this type of review builds and nurtures participants' motivation and commitment to the unit's mission and goals[9]

In addition, by addressing the success of a unit (and its potential weaknesses), strategic planning directly affects future planning decisions. Individuals participating in the strategic planning process must be made aware of these three benefits. Finally, Bryson notes that strategic planning can also help to "facilitate communication, participation, and judgments; accommodate divergent interests and values; foster wise decision making informed by reasonable analysis; promote successful implementation and accountability; and enhance ongoing learning."[10]

Although strategic planning has the advantage of creating a "well-constructed and conducted evaluation [that] is a service to the organization, its stakeholders, and its clients,"[11] this process includes challenges. First and foremost, strategic planning takes time. In an ideal world, organizations would hire consultants to assist those leading the strategic planning process, but this rarely is the case. Thus, it is imperative to identify the optimal time for beginning the strategic planning process by charting the ebb and flow of the unit. For fellowships advisors, most downtime—if it exists at all—is likely to be in the summer months, so this can be an ideal time to begin the strategic planning process. Advisors will want to take advantage of those on campus with strategic planning expertise, as they might be willing to walk the unit through the beginning of the process, alleviating some of the initial stress. Another challenge related to the time involved with strategic planning is the fact that strategic planning must occur alongside everyday tasks. It can be incredibly stressful trying to forecast how a unit will succeed in five years when the advisor is simply worried about recruiting for the upcoming award cycle. For those who are mandated to participate in strategic planning, not understanding the benefit of the process can also be a challenge. Remembering the individual benefits Sergiovanni listed above may help most overcome this challenge.

Two remaining challenges are related to the organization's communication style and willingness to take action. Unfortunately, some staff and faculty may have a general distrust of any administrative mandate, and the strategic planning process may be interpreted as a way for the administration to impose its hidden agenda. Organizations can help circumvent this belief by communicating directly about the reason for engaging in strategic planning and, most importantly, how the final results of the plan will be used and where they will be published. One of the most frustrating challenges associated with strategic planning is when individual units create assessment plans, conduct programmatic reviews, and develop a strategic plan only to see that plan be submitted and never referenced again. Even if this is the case, however, an individual unit can still reap the benefits by implementing the new plan.

Strategic Planning Components

Possessing a basic understanding of the benefits and challenges of strategic planning will assist those new to the process. A strategic plan is comprised of seven main components that operate individually and holistically (Figure 7.2).

Once participants acquire a basic understanding of the strategic planning components, the next step is to develop a timeline for the process. The timeline is divided into four sections and, depending on participants' knowledge of campus culture and of their own unit, the first three sections may take anywhere from one to four weeks to complete (Table 7.1).

Although it is presented here as such, the strategic planning timeline is not necessarily linear; that is, an individual or group may want to begin by reviewing the organization's mission and vision statements and then create or adjust their own mission and vision statements before discussing strategic issues. This deviation from the timeline is perfectly acceptable as the strategic planning process must be adapted to those engaging in the practice. The first two sections present areas to address that can be fairly easy to answer; however, those new to strategic planning may find the

Figure 7.2. Overview of Strategic Planning Components[12]

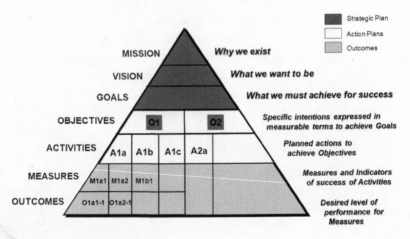

Table 7.1. Strategic Planning Timeline[13]

Phase I			Phase II	Phase III
Determine Position	Develop Strategy		Create the Plan	Manage the Plan
1–4 weeks	1–4 weeks		1–2 weeks	Ongoing
Strategic Issues: Identify strategic issues to address (e.g., how to increase outreach).	**Mission/Values:** Determine your unit's core purpose, especially as it relates to the institution's mission, and beliefs (cf. NAFA's Core Values).		**Review Institution's Strategic Plan:** Identify points of overlap between your unit and the college/university.	**Rollout:** Establish schedule for data collection and progress reviews and communicate strategy to entire unit and reporting lines.
Fellowship/Scholarship Data: Identify fellowship opportunities (e.g., increase in students receiving Pell Grants) and threats (e.g., other activities drawing upon potential applicants' time)	**Vision:** Create a description of your unit's indicators of success five years from now		**Use SWOT:** Revisit the SWOT analysis to set priorities.	**Data Collection:** Begin measuring outcomes.
User Insights: Contemplate current user satisfaction and identify future demand.	**Competitive Advantages:** Solidify your unique position.		**Outcomes/Measures:** Create SMART Goals.	**Adapt Quarterly:** Hold progress reviews and modify plan.
SWOT Analysis: Synthesize data into SWOT items.	**Long-Term Objectives:** Develop a five-year balanced framework that contains six objectives or less.		**Budget:** Align budget with the plan.	**Update Annually:** Review all measures and plan; update as needed.

University of Michigan's strategic planning questions especially helpful when beginning the process (Table 7.2).

The most important document to emerge from Phase I "determining position" is the SWOT analysis. The SWOT analysis need not be a formal document, complete with data from an organization's peer or aspirational

Table 7.2. Strategic Planning Questions Adapted from the University of Michigan[14]

1. What are the most significant strengths of your unit? What are the most important things that you could do to build those strengths?
2. What are the most worrisome weaknesses within your unit? What are the most important things you could do to shore them up?
3. What are the directions in which your best competitors are headed? How do these directions compare to the direction in which your unit is headed? What will set you apart from the crowd yet distinguish you among your peer schools?
4. What are the comparative advantages or definitive strengths of your unit at your college/university, relative to the very best schools or universities within your field across the nation and the world? What does your college/university give you as an advantage? What collaborations and activities within other units of your college/university would you like to see emerge in the next few years?
5. How can you exploit collaborations in the furtherance of your goals? What do you need elsewhere in the college/university to reach your goals?
6. What do want your unit to look like in ten years?
7. What implications do your plans have for undergraduate education? Graduate and professional education?
8. How do your goals enhance your unit's educational values?
9. What implications do your plans have for collaborations here and elsewhere?
10. What are the implications for increased outreach and public service?
11. Diversity, along many dimensions, remains an important goal of the college/university. How will your plans enhance the diversity within the unit, within the profession, and within the college/university?

Table 7.3. SWOT Analysis

Strengths	Weaknesses
• What do you do well? • What are your advantages? • What do you do better than others? • What relevant resources do you have? • What unique capabilities do you possess? • What do others perceive as your strengths?	• How can you improve your offerings? • What do you do poorly, or not at all? • What can you improve on given the current situation? • Is your budget enough to cover your needs? • What do others perceive as your weaknesses?
Opportunities	*Threats*
• Which trends or conditions may positively impact you? • What is the best period of the year for you to offer your services? • Can you enlarge your service area? • Can you increase media coverage surrounding your services/ outcomes?	• Which trends or conditions may negatively impact you? • What is the worst period of the year to promote your services and why? • What are your competitors doing that may impact you? • How do your weaknesses impact your threats?

institutions. It may be enough for members of the unit to begin by brainstorming answers to the questions in each area in order to create a table that addresses each area in a separate quadrant (Table 7.3).

Most individuals have no difficulty distinguishing between mission and vision statements and are able to complete the first two sections of the timeline fairly easily; however, some encounter difficulties when trying to differentiate between goals and objectives, objectives and measures, and measures and outcomes. For example, it is likely that most fellowship offices have a *goal* of increasing their number of scholarship applicants each year since an increase in applicants most likely ties in with the organization's mission or value statements in some manner. To translate that goal into an *objective*, a fellowship office could state that it plans to increase applicants by 2 percent each year. To achieve that goal, the fellowship office will then need to identify *activities* to accomplish that objective, such as hosting additional information sessions in the evenings and weekends. The *measure* of that activity will be the number of students who attend the additional information sessions, and the *outcome* would be the percentage of those attendees who apply for an award.

Although having a fully developed assessment plan results in a more effective strategic plan, units may still engage in the strategic planning process by identifying specific goals that result from their mission and vision statements and then rewriting those goals using the SMART format (Table 7.4).

Strategic Planning Materials

Once the strategic plan has been completed, next consider how to present the plan to and engage with stakeholders. Stakeholders are "any person, group, or organization that can place a claim on an organization's attention, resources, or output or that is affected by that output."[15] *Primary* or *key stakeholders* are usually internal actors who engage with the office directly and wield the most authority or influence, whereas *secondary stakeholders* are usually internal actors who engage with the office indirectly. *Tertiary stakeholders* are external actors who do not make decisions about the office or benefit from the office's operations but have the ability to influence the office's decisions (it might be helpful to think of this group as advocates).

The most important stakeholders are the office's primary or key stakeholders, and great care must be taken to identify these individuals or groups. Kenny presents a very clear set of questions to assist individuals in identifying primary and key stakeholders: (1) Does the individual have a fundamental impact on your organization's performance? Required response: Yes; (2) Can the office clearly identify what it needs from the individual? Required response: Yes; (3) Is the relationship dynamic (i.e., Does the office want the relationship to grow? If so, is the relationship able to grow)? Required response: Yes; (4) Can the office exist without or easily replace the individual? Required response: No; and (5) Has the

Table 7.4. Using the **SMART** Format

Example:	Given the importance of applicants' willingness to self-disclose when applying for fellowships, two weeks after participating in a personal statement writing workshop, 80 percent of randomly selected participants will report a 20 percent increase in their willingness to communicate via the online completion of the Willingness to Communicate Scale.
Specific	This outcome identifies who is involved (randomly selected personal statement writing workshop participants), what is being measured (participants' willingness to communicate), where (online), when the measurement will occur (two weeks after the workshop), and why (being comfortable self-disclosing assists applicants in writing more effective personal statements).
Measurable	The Willingness to Communicate Scale measures how likely one is to initiate and continue communicating in a variety of contexts. The face validity of the instrument is strong, and results of extensive research indicate the predictive validity of the instrument.
Achievable	Reviewing past research, a reported increase of 20 percent could be attributable to participation in the workshop.
Relevant	Since personal statements are an essential component of fellowship/scholarship applications, applicants' willingness to communicate about themselves is imperative.
Time-bound	Administering the measure two weeks after the workshop will downplay the primacy-recency effect.

individual already been identified through another relationship? Required response: No.[16]

Once primary stakeholders have been identified, secondary and tertiary stakeholders should be identified next. The simplest way to classify stakeholders at this point is by using the stakeholder management matrix (Table 7.5).

Table 7.5. Stakeholder Management Matrix[17]

HIGH	Friends	Champions
	• Maintain communication about project. • Employ as ambassadors for the project.	• Find ways to maintain constant face-to-face contact. • Involve in project role. • Involve to facilitate change. • Ascertain their key needs and expectations.
Level of Support	Onlookers	Blockers
	• Maintain communication about project. • Show disadvantages of failure to support. • Do not waste resources on these groups.	• Understand their resistance and put in place steps to remove threats. • Provide information about projects. • Explore and show benefits of project. • Maintain constant contact to build relationships.
LOW	**Potential Impact**	HIGH

Given the usefulness of reviewing the matrix in practice, I have included the initial matrix I created based on my initial impressions of the university (Table 7.6).

Once a unit has identified the three types of stakeholders, the final step is to determine how to interact with chosen allies. The University of Kansas Center for Community Health and Development has created an Ally Power Grid to assist individuals in clarifying the power(s) a potential ally might wield to assist a given unit.[18] Completing this grid will help units identify which allies are the most powerful. As is the case with the Stakeholder Management Matrix completed by the author above, the example of the completed Ally Power Grid is tailored to the author's university (Table 7.7). Completing the Ally Power Grid is the final step in the initial phase of the strategic planning process. Of course, units will need

Table 7.6. Author's Example of Stakeholder Classification

	Friends (High Influence & Low Interest) Keep Satisfied & Educate	*Champions* (High Influence & High Interest) Manage Closely
HIGH	• President • Deans • Alumni • Greek Life • Speaker's Lab	• Provost • Dept. Chairs (most) • Center for Citizenship & Community • Center for Urban Ecology • Writers' Studio	• Faculty Selection Committees • Study Abroad Office • Associate Deans • Previous Recommendation Writers • Student Affairs	• Award Recipients • SGA Officers/Clubs • Faculty Award Recipients • Career Services • Butler Summer Institute • Faculty Mentors
Level of Support	*Onlookers* (Low Influence & Low Interest) Monitor	*Blockers* (Low Influence & Low Interest) Keep Informed
	• Faculty Senate	• School of Business* • Program directors who feel my funding takes away from their offices	• College of Education* • Those who feel fellowships are elitist
LOW		
	Potential Impact	**HIGH**

*These are great individuals, but they want their majors to graduate and immediately enter the job market or begin teaching; some faculty in these colleges are not interested in helping recruit per se.

Table 7.7. Author's Example of Complete Ally Power Grid

Type of Power	Rationale	Example	What Could They Do?	What Would They Expect in Return?	Engagement Strategy?
Members: How many members does the group have?	The more members a group has, the less likely it is to be ignored	• Faculty Senate (S) • Dept Chair Forum (S) • Student Government Assoc/ Groups (S)	Recruit Publicize Recipients	Acknowledgment Publicity	Attend Meetings Monthly Updates
Money: Will they donate money to your issue?	Donated money and other resources are always welcome in achieving your group's goals.	• Administrators (P) • Donors (S) • Alumni (S)	Generate Other Awards Recruit Publicize Recipients	Acknowledgment Publicity	Yearly Informal Meeting (hors d'oeuvres)
Credibility: Do they bring special credibility?	A group with strong positive recognition in your community will help bring credibility to your own group.	• Faculty (P) • Award Recipients (S) • Center for Faith and Vocation (S) • Center for Urban Ecology (S)	Recruit Publicize Recipients	Acknowledgment Publicity	Monthly Updates
Appeal: Do they have special appeal?	Some groups of people have universal appeal, and if your group is connected to them, it will help your image as well.	• Teaching Award Recipients (P/S) • Research Award Recipients (P/S) • Donors (P/S/T) • Alumni (P/S/T)	Recruit Publicize Recipients	Acknowledgment Publicity	One on One Meetings Yearly Updates

Criterion	Description	Stakeholders			
Network: Are they part of a large, organized network?	A group that has lots of other groups in its network is going to have financial resources, credibility, and some political power.	• Honors Program (S) • Student Government Assoc (S) • Greek Life (S) • Financial Aid (S) • Student Affairs (S)	Recruit Publicize Recipients Procure Information	Publicity Acknowledgment	Attend Meetings Yearly Update
Reputation: Do they have a reputation for toughness?	Groups with a tough reputation may discourage opponents.	• Departments (S) • Center for Citizenship and Community (S) • Center for Global Education (S)	Recruit Publicize Recipients	Publicity Acknowledgment	Attend Meetings Yearly Update
Skills: Do they have special skills?	An ally may bring technical, business, or legal skills to your group.	• Career Services (S) • Writing/Speaking Centers (S) • Butler Summer Institute (S)	Recruit Publicize Recipients	Publicity Acknowledgment	One on One Meetings Monthly Updates Yearly Update
Newsworthy: Are they particularly newsworthy?	Some groups may have a reputation or connections in the media that make them newsworthy. If they align with you, that might bring you positive media attention.	• Departments (S) • Marketing/Communications (S)	Recruit Publicize Recipients	Publicity Acknowledgment	Yearly Update

P = Primary Stakeholder, S = Secondary Stakeholder, T = Tertiary Stakeholder to engage in data collection, quarterly review, and annual review to ensure that the strategic plan remains valid.

The strategic planning process, while essential for programs to function at optimal levels, can be intimidating and overwhelming. For those new to the strategic planning process, the steps outlined above should assist fellowships advisors in considering their role on campus and how best to improve the ways our offices interact with students, operate on our campuses, and—most importantly—demonstrate the value of scholarship advising services. Those with strategic planning experience, including all the components discussed above, should offer additional perspectives perhaps not previously considered. Whether fellowships advisors complete the first two phases of strategic planning on their own or with the assistance of others, enacting the plan and communicating the results generated from objectives identified in the plan will highlight how fellowships advising offices are central to a college or university's mission.

Notes

1. "Survey of the Profession 2017," in *Roads Less Traveled and Other Perspectives on Nationally Competitive Scholarships*, eds. Suzanne McCray and Joanne Brzinski (Fayetteville: University of Arkansas Press, 2017), 178–79.

2. Ibid.

3. John M. Bryson, *Strategic Planning for Public and Nonprofit Organizations*, 5th ed. (Hoboken, NJ: John Wiley & Sons, 2018), 8.

4. Bryson, *Strategic Planning*, 35–36.

5. For more information on the programmatic review process, see Dacia Charlesworth, "Demystifying the Programmatic Review Process: Ensuring Quality Control, Fostering Faculty Development, and Motivating Faculty," in *A Communication Assessment Primer*, eds. Phil Backlund and Gay Wakefield (Washington, DC: National Communication Association, 2010), 95–106, https://www.natcom.org/sites/default/files/pages/Assessment_Resources_A _Communication_Assessment_Primer.pdf.

6. Chicago State University, "Strategic Planning Resources," http://www .csu.edu/strategicplanningresources/planningcycle.htm.

7. *Oxford English Dictionary*, 3rd ed. (Oxford: Oxford University Press, 2010), s.v. "Review."

8. Francis Gouillart, "The Day the Music Died," *Journal of Business Strategy* 16, no. 3 (1995): 14–20.

9. Thomas J. Sergiovanni, *The Principalship: A Reflective Practice Perspective* (Toronto: Allyn & Bacon., 1987).

10. Bryson, *Strategic Planning*, 9–10.

11. Bruce Hendricks, "Moving Ahead: Program Review and Evaluation as Tools for Growth," *Proceedings of the 1992 and 1993 Conferences on Outdoor Recreation* (1992–1993), 65.

12. Steve Matthews, "Strategic Planning Components," *21st Century Library* blog, June 4, 2010, https://21stcenturylibrary.com/page/48/.

13. This timeline is adapted from "Our Strategy Management Process," OnStrategy, https://onstrategyhq.com/resources/strategic-planning-process -basics.

14. University of Michigan, "Strategic Planning Process and Detail Document," https://www.provost.umich.edu/programs/strategic_assessment /Strategic%20Assessment%20Process.pdf.

15. Bryson, *Strategic Planning*, 42.

16. Graham Kenny, "Five Questions to Identify Key Stakeholders," *Harvard Business Review*, March 6, 2014, https://hbr.org/2014/03/five-questions-to -identify-key-stakeholders.

17. This map is based on a table included in Andrew Kumar's article "Client and Stakeholder Engagement: Tools and Techniques," October 7, 2015, https:// medium.com/@kumar/client-and-stakeholder-engagement-tools-and-techniques -3fee33c82f26.

18. University of Kansas Center for Community Health and Development, "Ally Power Grid," https://ctb.ku.edu/en/table-of-contents/advocacy/advocacy -principles/recognize-allies/tools.

8

How Do Graduate Students Search for Fellowships and Grants? Why Knowing Matters

TERESA DELCORSO-ELLMANN

Teresa Delcorso-Ellmann *is assistant dean in the Graduate School, New Brunswick, and founding director of GradFund, the Resource Center for Graduate Student External Support.*

For the past twenty years, her work at Rutgers University has focused on helping students and scholars develop program and research plans. Her career with the university began in the Edward J. Bloustein School of Planning and Public Policy dean's office, where she ran the school's Career Development office and Hubert H. Humphrey Fellowship Program. After three years in the Bloustein School, she began to work in the field of external grants and fellowships with the Department of Sociology and the FAS dean's office, where she was research coordinator for the Center for Social Research and Instruction.

In 2000, she joined the Graduate School, New Brunswick dean's office as founding director of GradFund, the Resource Center for Graduate Student External Support, a service dedicated to assisting graduate students in identifying and applying for external grants and fellowships. During her tenure with the GradFund, she has helped many graduate students secure merit-based research grants and fellowships. Delcorso-Ellmann has a BA in history and international affairs from the University of Mary Washington in Fredericksburg, Virginia, and an MA in history from Rutgers, Newark.

The fellowship and grant universe for graduate students offers a robust selection of awards, large and small. Some of these national awards are well known, with extensive information readily available to graduate students. Many small, lesser-known awards cater to the needs of graduate students in a specific discipline or research area. Indeed, the landscape is complex and can be a challenge for graduate students to navigate. Many graduate students learn about relevant funding opportunities thanks to the outreach efforts of the fellowships advising office on campus. Additionally, students will typically receive information on upcoming competitions through discipline-specific listservs. As fellowships advisors frame their work with graduate students as a student-centered, professional development activity, two important questions to consider are *how graduate students search for fellowships and grants* and *how fellowships advisors can guide them through the search and selection process.*[1]

Looking closely at graduate students' fellowship search goals is a key place to begin, followed by a data analysis that bears both on what graduate students do in their searches and on how advisors might better help them achieve their objectives. For doctoral students, applying for funding is an important part of building their scholarly, discipline-based identity. As such, applying for and securing research funds plays an important role not only in providing resources for their research, but also for building their curriculum vita (CV) and facilitating their entry into the discipline. When coaching students through their list of resources, the narrative shared with them should go beyond helping them meet the need for resources and discuss how their research aligns with the institutional priorities of a specific funder and discipline. For example, biomedical students need to understand how National Institutes of Health (NIH) funding could help build career pathways for them as a biomedical researcher. Likewise, humanities students should know that a Mellon could be both a financial resource and an important recognition of the broad humanistic significance of their work to their discipline and the humanities writ large.

Mentoring graduate students through the process of searching for and selecting funding opportunities is an important role. As graduate students pursue their research, an important part of their training is to learn about the research enterprise, broadly defined, including the key funders who will support their work as a graduate student and beyond. Many universities subscribe to research-funding databases such as Pivot, SPIN, and GrantForward. Additionally, many graduate schools support their own in-house database of graduate student awards. While these tools should be useful to graduate students and provide them with a basic understanding of funding options, frequently students report frustration with the search interfaces and results. Graduate students who learn how to navigate these funders while completing their graduate training will enter their research career with a greater fluency in grantsmanship, which in turn will help increase their research profile. As such, it is useful for graduate fellowships advisors to better understand how graduate students search for and identify research funds, so advisors can help students connect research interests to the appropriate funder.

Graduate fellowship applicants are at a unique stage of their scholarly and professional development. Depending on whether they are pursuing a master's degree or doctoral degree, their professional goals and ambitions are intrinsically linked to their motivations and approaches to applying for grants and fellowships. Master's students, for example, fall into two distinct groups: students who are pursuing either a research-based master's degree or a professional master's degree. The master's track for the student determines which fellowships and grants the student should consider. When students pursue a research-based degree and aspire to go on to a doctoral program, securing research funding as master's students can raise their profile as they apply to doctoral programs. At the same time, if students plan to go on to a doctoral degree, they need to think strategically about the most opportune moments to apply for certain graduate-level awards. As in the case of the National Science Foundation Graduate Research Fellowship Program (NSF GRFP), master's support lasts two years and doctoral support three, and it will be more advantageous to position their application so they can maximize the doctoral-level benefits of the award. If students are successful with the NSF GRFP, there is a compelling argument that they should use the three years of support for doctoral work. A professional master's degree will not typically involve research, and this in turn will limit the number of awards available to support professional master's students. Nonetheless, there are some important awards such as the Fulbright, which can be a useful post-master's gap year support. Or as in the case of the Boren and SMART programs, the grant can be an important award mechanism to help students achieve their career goals of securing employment in government service

Aside from master's degrees and the PhD, postgraduate students may seek out other external fellowships, including those in professional doctoral programs such as PsyD, DMA, and DPT. Additionally, it is possible that students pursuing a JD, MD, or DDS will also seek out information on fellowships and grants. The graduate-level fellowships advisor needs to understand the complex landscape of graduate degrees and career pathways as well as how grants and fellowships can most effectively support students in different graduate degree programs.

For doctoral students, applying for external grants and fellowships is a central part of their professional development. Indeed, any individual pursuing a PhD and a research career should incorporate into their course of study training in the basic skills of identifying and applying for funding. As such, supporting the application process from developing ideas to identifying relevant funders and developing competitive applications should be framed as a team-based approach that will include the doctoral student, the advisor, faculty mentors, administrative and business professionals in their graduate program or research center, and professionals such as graduate fellowships advisors and research development professionals.

For doctoral students, the disciplinary concerns of their PhD program take precedence. Students are engaged in deep, immersive professional development experiences as they master scholarly content and engage in the analysis and critique of that content with the goal of developing projects that will build the field through innovation, theory development, and the production of new knowledge. Importantly, hand in hand with their development as scholars, graduate students are cultivating a scholarly identity as they prepare to join the professoriate or other professional careers. In this enterprise, which is both high risk and high gain, there are many places in the journey where students run the risk of departing from their planned course of study. As a doctoral candidate, the student is involved in the process of identity formation as a scholar and professional peer.

Integrated into the discourse of what it means to be a scholar in a specific field is a discussion of the key funders that will support the research and scholarship that the graduate student plans to undertake. This conversation intersects with discussions about professional development in the scholarly field and identity in a research subspecialty as well as larger discussions about funding in the higher education enterprise and who pays for the research that faculty undertake. For those who are faculty in training, it is essential they complete their degrees with core competencies in the funding landscape for their research area. Importantly, the funding that a graduate student can apply for is driven not exclusively by their specific scholarly agenda but more frequently by their research field.

For doctoral students, their faculty mentor, or principal investigator (PI), is their key partner in their doctoral work. The relationship should be a mentoring one, but it can also be very hierarchical, and the expectation is that the student, while under the guidance of an advisor, will work closely with the advisor, following instructions and modeling both research and grant-writing best practices. Depending on the advisor-advisee relationship and the disciplinary norms that govern their work, the graduate student may work very independently or with a high degree of supervision from the research mentor. The nature of the relationship will influence how the student engages with the process of applying for funding.

Applying for funding is time-consuming and challenging, and for the novice applicant, there may be a steep and daunting learning curve. The proposal-writing genre is a crucial skill that graduate students should develop while they are in graduate school. Proposal writing is a unique genre, different from the writing style they are mastering as PhD students, and some students may be reluctant to develop yet another form of scholarly writing. Advisors need to emphasize to graduate students that proposal writing is indeed a form of scholarly writing and a goal they should embrace while they are graduate students to develop a scholarly communication toolkit that will include developing not just the disciplinary writing of seminar papers, conference papers, journal articles and manuscripts, but also proposal writing. However, applying for funding is more than writing the proposal; it is first identifying the relevant award, determining the best time to apply, learning about the fellowship or grant, and then tailoring the application materials to the specific funder while compiling and completing the required supporting paperwork.

An effective strategy for graduate students to use to frame their search for funding is to think about how to integrate the application process into their graduate career. The timing of fellowship and grant application deadlines, notification, and award activation frequently do not map neatly to the student study timelines. By casting this challenge as an opportunity to integrate applying for funding into their graduate career, two important goals are achieved. First, they make the process of searching for funding opportunities and then applying for them an integral part of their research process. Second, they have a framework to help them align their plan of graduate study and the application process.

Many doctoral students will have a funding package to support their program of study. This funding package can include fellowship support or teaching or research assistantships. In order to motivate these students to apply for funding, the advisor may need to encourage them to think about how to integrate external funding with their internal package. The internal pressures they face from their graduate program and graduate school can also have an impact on their motivations to apply for external funding. These internal pressures may include the possibility of losing internal funding should they receive external funds or the need to stay on track for a time-to-degree requirement.

STEM students are typically required to complete an individual development plan (IDP) as a part of their professional development activities. In this plan, students map out their course of study, a research plan, professional development goals, and graduate student activities. Applying for external funding should also be included in the plan and can cultivate the idea of integrating applying for funding into the graduate career. Even if students are not required to develop a plan, they should be encouraged to do so, or at the very least, to develop a funding plan to map out the grants and fellowships that they will apply for over the course of their graduate studies.

There are a number of resources to help graduate students identify and apply for external funding. Indeed, an important role for the graduate fellowships advisor is to assist students in understanding how to best use these multiple resources and to maximize the efficacy of resources that originate from the central administration, program level, disciplinary or research focus areas, or from outside of the university.

Depending on the institutional setting, there may be a number of different resources to which the graduate student has access, and understanding how and when to use them can be confusing. Importantly, graduate students often hold multiple roles in their university setting. They will all be students, but depending on their source of institutional support, they may also be considered employees. Additionally, some funders will consider them to be a PI or Co-PI and will require that they process their grant submission through the university's sponsored research office. This activity in particular is important not just for the processing of the application, but also for student development as it may be the student's first foray into working with the professional research development staff in the university.

There are a number of subscription-based grant and fellowship database services that exist, and most universities subscribe to one or more of them. Exemplars include the Foundation Center Directory, COS/PIVOT, GrantForward, SPIN, and IRIS. The institutional decision to subscribe to one or more of these databases is usually made at a high level, and there can be a number of challenges. The first challenge is which product to subscribe to and how useful it will be to the user community. In this evaluation, a real question is whether or not the needs of graduate students are considered in the evaluation. They may or may not be, depending on the institutional context. Regardless of the product, most of these are geared to institutional and faculty researchers. While the databases often include information for graduate students, the information may not be optimized for the graduate student user who is new to searching for grants and fellowships and is in the early stages of developing their scholarly research identity, shaping how they understand the practice of applying for research funds. Another issue is that, as with any subscription-based service, the university may decide to switch providers. While there may be good reasons for this, depending on when the change occurs in an individual graduate student's tenure, such changes could be highly disruptive in terms of the learning curve about the varying external funding and the mastery of a new technological tool. In general, challenges with subscription-based resources affect both faculty and graduate students and include the ineffectual searches that can result and the need to digest and sort through a massive amount of information and detail. New users can find assessing what is valuable information to be unmanageable.

Given the challenges of subscription-based databases and the unique needs of graduate students, many graduate advising offices create their own, proprietary, graduate-specific funding databases. These resources can be the most useful for graduate students because they are developed and maintained by graduate fellowships advising professionals. The challenge is that creating this type of resource takes time, expertise, and money and may not be feasible for every advising office. There are a number of excellent, graduate student–focused resources, which are available to all graduate students, including those at Rutgers University (GradFund), University of Illinois, University of California Los Angeles, and Cornell University.

The graduate funding landscape is a complicated one. Driven by the funder visions and goals for the development of young professionals and scholars in a postbaccalaureate setting, the opportunities and their eligibility requirements, application rules, and review processes can seem unwieldy or excessively complicated to students with no discernable patterns. Advisors, on the other hand, understand the many resources available to students and their faculty mentors that can help identify fellowship and grant opportunities. But understanding how graduate students search for funding and how *they* understand the opportunities available to them is important for advisors to know in order to make sure students do not miss out on opportunities that could support their work. To ascertain how to most effectively mentor and guide graduate students through the process of learning how to search for relevant grants and fellowships, our office tracked and analyzed the search terms used on the GradFund database over a twelve-month period, from November 2015 to November 2016.

The GradFund Database search interface (Figure 8.1) is a basic one. Users can enter a keyword or a set of keywords, much like a Google search, or they can use a combination of search filters. The search mechanism uses keywords to search through the grant and fellowship descriptions, while the search filters correspond to the back-end coding of the award records.

Our office conducted the research through Google Analytics, embedded on the search page to keep track of search interface behavior, depth of exploration, and complexity of a particular search. We also analyzed the breakdown of typed search terms into categories as well as evaluated how the drop-down menu items impacted the award search. Finally, we tracked the page views for awards and funders, analyzing which funding options received more attention from students.

When using the manual search option, the majority of students (44 percent) searched the award database using research topic–related

Figure 8.1. GradFund Database Search Interface

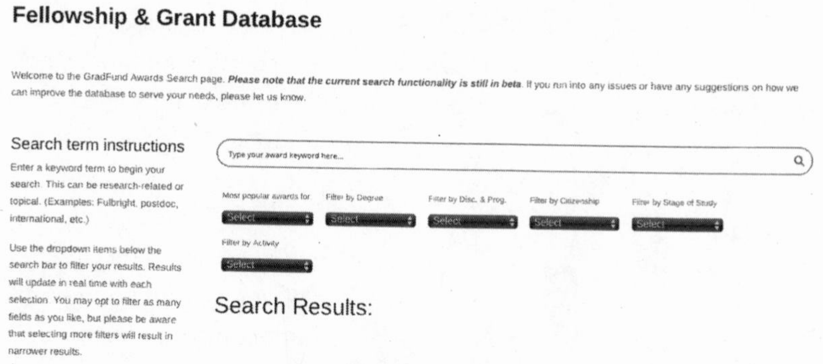

Fellowship & Grant Database

Welcome to the GradFund Awards Search page. *Please note that the current search functionality is still in beta.* If you run into any issues or have any suggestions on how we can improve the database to serve your needs, please let us know.

Search term instructions

Enter a keyword term to begin your
search. This can be research-related or
topical. (Examples: Fulbright, postdoc,
international, etc.)

Use the dropdown items below the
search bar to filter your results. Results
will update in real time with each
selection. You may opt to filter as many
fields as you like, but please be aware
that selecting more filters will result in
narrower results.

Type your award keyword here...

Most popular awards for   Filter by Degree   Filter by Disc. & Prog.   Filter by Citizenship   Filter by Stage of Study

Select   Select   Select   Select   Select

Filter by Activity

Select

Search Results:

search terms rather than those associated with their discipline or graduate program. When students were guided by drop-down menus to filter the results, the majority (49 percent) searched by activity funded. Importantly, students generally did not look beyond the first page of the search results, with the number of viewers significantly dropping beyond the initial page (from 8,322 unique page views for the first page to 329 unique views on the second page).

In the analysis of the searches done by students (Figure 8.2), both guided by the filters and in the free-form search box, the category most frequently searched was activity funded, followed by graduate program, research topic, and stage of study. Student users frequently reported frustrations with the search results they encountered and reported that they could not find anything to meet their needs. When we examine the search behavior by the students who only used the search filters (Figure 8.3), the results are similar. Most users search by activity and then by discipline.

The results of this study have helped our office better understand how students search for funding and, more importantly, how they understand grants and fellowships, both in function and in support. Importantly for us as graduate fellowships advisors, we better understand how to redefine the underlying taxonomies of our database and how to present and explain to graduate students and their faculty mentors the graduate funding landscape, the opportunities it presents to graduate students regardless of discipline or degree program, and how to more effectively integrate applying for funding into a graduate career.

Figure 8.2. Category Searched, both Typed and Guided

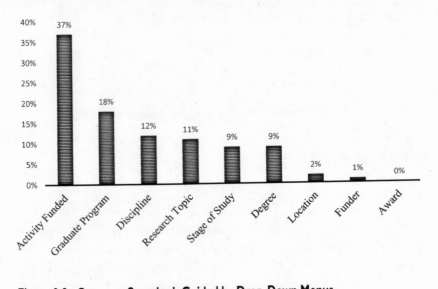

Figure 8.3. Category Searched, Guided by Drop-Down Menus

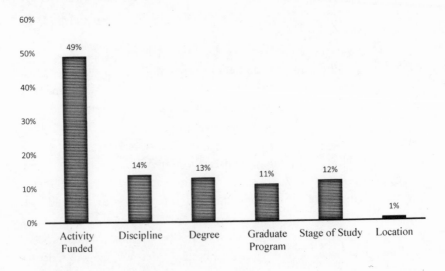

Based on our study of graduate student search behavior and our fol-
low-up analysis of the GradFund database of over three thousand awards,
we developed two taxonomies to define the graduate funding landscape:
stage of graduate study (Table 8.1) and disciplinary focus (Table 8.2).
The stage-of-study framework includes nine categories that start out as a

Table 8.1. Defining the Graduate Funding Landscape: Stage of Graduate Study

Stage of Study	Definition
Postgraduate	Provides support to students in a variety of graduate-level programs (e.g., master's, doctoral, research, professional arts)
Cross-Stage Support	Provides support to students in research-based graduate degree programs. The award may be applied for and utilized at various stages of graduate study, including master's level.
Master's Support	Provides support specifically for students pursuing either a research or professional master's degree
Early Graduate/ Pre-dissertation	Provides support to early-career doctoral students who will typically be eligible to apply in years one and two of their doctoral program
Dissertation Research	Provides support specifically for the research stage of the doctoral degree. The funder typically requires that the applicant be ABD to apply for or to receive funding.
Dissertation Research & Writing	Provides support to doctoral students to assist with research and/or writing tasks of the dissertation. The funder typically requires that the applicant be ABD to apply for or to receive funding.
Dissertation Writing/ Completion	Provides support for the final year of writing the PhD. The funder typically requires that the applicant is ABD to be eligible to apply and will need to demonstrate that they are far enough along with their doctoral work to complete the degree requirements during the fellowship year.
Predoctoral/ Postdoctoral	Provides support at either the dissertation or postdoctoral stage or is an award designed to provide support for the researcher to complete their dissertation and then transition to a postdoctoral research position. The applicant will typically need to be ABD at the time of application or award.
Postdoctoral Support	Provides fellowship support for a postdoctoral project. The applicant will typically need to be in the final stages of completing their PhD or to be a newly minted PhD.

Table 8.2. Disciplinary Focus Taxonomy

Disciplines in the GradFund Database	Degrees Represented
STEM Fields	
Biological Sciences	Research doctorate and master's, professional master's
Biomedical Sciences	Research doctorate and master's, professional master's
Physical, Mathematical Sciences, and Engineering	Research doctorate and master's, professional master's
Social Sciences	Research doctorate and master's, professional master's, professional doctorate
Non-STEM Fields	
Humanities	Research doctorate and master's, professional master's
Visual, Performing, and Creative Arts	Research doctorate and master's, professional master's, professional doctorate

general classification for postgraduate work that can include master's and doctoral work, research, and practitioner degrees. This information builds out to specifically focus on doctoral work and the key stages of study as students work toward their PhD. One of our goals is to help graduate students understand the importance of stage of study in defining the fellowships and grants that they are currently eligible to apply for and that may be awards they can apply for in the future.

Analyzing the awards through a stage of graduate study framework helped us to quickly identify awards that would be appropriate for professional degree programs, separate from the many awards that support research degrees. Awards categorized as postgraduate are open to students pursuing any type of postgraduate degree, while awards categorized as cross-stage support are specifically for students pursuing a research-based graduate degree. Importantly, there are many cross-stage support awards available to students who may be pursuing a research-based master's or doctoral degree. These awards will tend to be small awards and field or research topic specific. By bringing to the fore the importance of stage of study, we seek to help students focus on the awards most relevant to the degree program they are pursuing.

The second taxonomy we created was disciplinary focus, which is based on the disciplinary clusters in the Rutgers School of Graduate Studies. Our analysis of the search patterns of our users showed that through the free-form search of activity funded, most students were using search terms highly specific to their research topic. Our goal in redeveloping the disciplinary focus taxonomy was first to align with the disciplinary clusters in the newly created School of Graduate Studies, and second to provide students with a logical entry point to searching for funding in a way that connects meaningfully with their scholarly or professional identity. Understanding the user's impulse to use search terms that are specific to their program of study, we needed a way to build a search framework that made sense to their graduate identity and would provide useful and accurate but not an overwhelming number of results. It would not be feasible to microcode each database entry to reflect the multitude of research topics that are studied in our more than eighty graduate programs. The coding time and expertise required far exceeded our capacities.

Rather than create a Google-like search where users can enter their unique and specific terms to find funding, we based the search on stage of study and disciplinary focus. The advantage of using disciplinary focus as a search anchor is that it connects with students' scholarly or professional identity and gives them the opportunity to see the broad range of awards open to their discipline.

The next stage in the project was to analyze the graduate student fellowships and grants in the GradFund database based on these two taxonomies. The analysis that follows is for awards with deadlines from May to December. While only a sample of the full database, this preliminary analysis highlights important data that can first better inform graduate advisors and second show graduate students how to more effectively search for and then integrate applying for funding into their graduate career.

The analysis of awards based on our stage-of-study taxonomy reveals interesting trends (see figure 8.4). First, over 30 percent of the awards are available to graduate students regardless of stage of study and degree program (postgraduate and cross-stage support). This subset of awards includes small, medium, and large research grants; small scholarships; and

Figure 8.4. Active Awards in the GradFund Database Based on Stage of Study (May to December Deadlines)

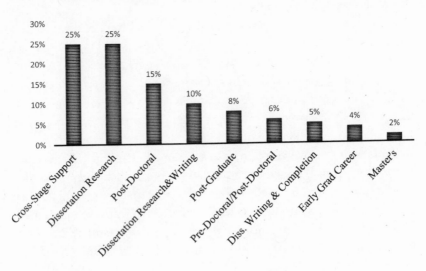

nine- to twelve-month fellowships. As many advisors work with master's students, more so than doctoral students, it is important to note that for most of these awards, both master's and doctoral students are eligible to apply. Additionally, a small percentage of awards are specifically for master's students. Importantly, though, 98 percent of the GradFund database contains awards for doctoral students, which is representative of the focus of the graduate funding landscape. As noted above, the postgraduate and cross-stage awards tend to be geared to students throughout their course of study. The remaining categories will require that the graduate student is at a specific stage of study. The early-career, pre-dissertation awards include the lucrative, multiyear fellowships. Doctoral awards (dissertation research, dissertation research and writing, dissertation writing/completion) require that the applicant be at a specific stage of study. The award portfolio includes research grants (small, medium, and large) and fellowship support for three to twelve months. At this stage, the awards are typically research site or topic specific.

The distribution of awards based on discipline favors STEM disciplines; however, 33 percent of the database awards are for the arts and humanities (see figure 8.5). Additionally, 23 percent of the awards are for the social sciences, which can range from STEM focused to humanities focused.

Figure 8.5. Active Awards Based on Disciplinary Focus (May to December Deadlines)

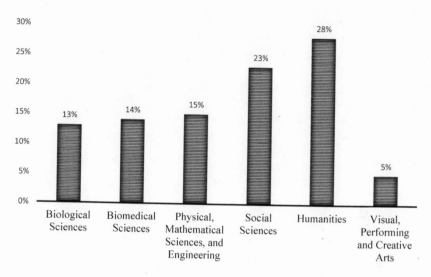

The analysis of the awards portfolio by stage of study and discipline provides important information to guide the advice and support advisors provide to graduate students, programs, and faculty. Importantly, there are many dissertation-level opportunities for graduate students in the humanities and social sciences to pursue. A more granular analysis will show how these opportunities map to specific research areas, which will help students better understand the opportunities available to them. In the STEM disciplines, there are a significant number of opportunities categorized as postgraduate or cross-stage, and the benefit of this is that these tend to be awards that students can apply for throughout their graduate careers. The issues raised here take advisors to a level of analytical complexity that may not have been previously reached and will likely be the basis of many future fruitful discussions in the graduate fellowships advising community.

Notes

1. The data and analysis on how graduate students use the GradFund search are the product of the collective effort of the GradFund Fellowships Advising Team. I would like to thank Sharon Baskind-Wing, Miya Carey,

Janna Ferguson, Senem Kaptan, Maria Elizabeth Roldan, and Kris White for their work on this project. Many thanks also go to Senem Kaptan for the early formulation and presentation on several of the ideas on how graduate students use the GradFund database. These ideas have also benefited from many conversations with the graduate fellowships advisor professional community, whose membership I would like to thank for their willingness to engage in collaborative discussions on how to better support our graduate students. Thanks in particular go to the participants in the 2018 NAFA regional conference on graduate advising, especially Samantha Lee, Kathryn Sawyer, Karen Rosenthall, Sarah Mehta, and Anne Janusch. A very special thank-you is extended to Stephen Ellmann for all of his support during every phase of this project.

Part III

International Awards

9

Fulbright 101
Developing a Fulbright Campus Culture

LAURA CLIPPARD

Laura Clippard has been honors college coordinator at Middle Tennessee
State University since 2008. She received a BS in psychology from East
Tennessee State University and an MS in human resource development from
the University of Tennessee, Knoxville. Her previous roles include serving
with three TRiO programs, Upward Bound, Educational Talent Search,
and Student Support Services, where she worked directly with low-income and
first-generation students. She is currently a member of the National
Association of Fellowships Advisors executive board and has been a national
reader for the Benjamin A. Gilman Scholarship, Critical Language
Scholarship (CLS), and Phi Kappa Phi (PKP) Study Abroad Scholarships.

My Journey as a Fulbright Program Advisor (FPA)

When I started as the FPA at Middle Tennessee State University (MTSU),
the Undergraduate Fellowships office was new, and my predecessor had

left the position several months prior to my start. My job duties at that time included being the sole honors college advisor to about eight hundred students, which required individual student meetings, leading honors college tours, traveling with admissions to out-of-town recruitment events for multiple days, and directing all international and national scholarship and fellowships advising and recruitment activities for a campus of twenty thousand students. Though the job seemed overwhelming, I received sound advice through the National Association of Fellowships Advisors (NAFA) on how to start with small steps to cultivate our Fulbright program.

Joanne Brzinski (Emory University) listened patiently as I described the many challenges and my own campus culture, and she helped me think critically about my plan of action for Fulbright. At many events connected with NAFA, I heard, "Focus on the process not the outcome. Help students grow professionally and learn about themselves through the application process." I asked questions on the NAFA listserv, asked more questions back on my campus, and was able to begin my own Fulbright journey. I discovered that my own values aligned well with the mission of Fulbright.

My first year, I read the Fulbright Program Advisor (FPA) manual from cover to cover and found this statement that struck me: "As outlined by Senator Fulbright, the purpose of the program is threefold:

1. To promote mutual understanding through a commitment to the free flow of ideas and people across national boundaries.
2. To expand, through this understanding, the boundaries of human wisdom, empathy and perception.
3. Through cooperation in constructive activities among people of different nations, to create true and lasting world peace."[1]

The words "lasting world peace" hit an emotional note with me. My mother-in-law was in Austria when it was occupied by the Nazi Party and sometimes shared those stories. In a world with political disagreements, Fulbright is about taking time to listen and understand those who are different from us. Fulbright gives students the chance to understand other cultures and to give back in a meaningful way.

My own interest helped with our Fulbright recruitment efforts. For example, while attending a MTSU TRiO event, I was able to discuss the Fulbright with many first-generation and low-income students, and one of the students decided to apply. She completed a Fulbright, became an active contributor to the foster care community from which she had come, and later attended Harvard Medical School. She wanted to give back to those who had believed in her, and thus fulfilled the mission of Fulbright to cultivate empathy and understanding.

In 2012, MTSU was recognized as a "Top Producing Fulbright Institute" in the *Chronicle of Higher Education*.[2] But regardless of the level of success with Fulbright, helping students complete the application is deeply rewarding. Even students who do not receive the Fulbright tell me that the application process allowed them to engage in deep reflection about who they are and why they are seeking their particular goals. On a practical level, they will sometimes use their Fulbright essays for graduate school or other fellowships, but they stress that the process of reflecting on their life journey is very gratifying.

No matter the overall number of student applications, all FPAs can develop a process to help their students with their life journeys, and FPAs can develop a campus culture that is friendly to Fulbright. This article discusses the various suggestions I have received over the years on how to assist students in developing competitive applications and how to structure a fellowship office to be student centered.

The Fulbright U.S. Student Program and the Benefits of Applying

The U.S. Fulbright Program, which was passed into law in 1946, allows U.S. citizens to serve as informal cultural ambassadors in other countries and brings citizens from other countries to the United States in a bilateral exchange. Senator J. William Fulbright used surplus war property to fund the "promotion of international good will through the exchange of students in the fields of education, culture, and science."[3] The idea behind the Fulbright Program was a simple concept: that nations need a better understanding of each other. The FPA works on the U.S. side of the exchange to encourage students to apply and helps them through the application and interview process.

Fulbright opportunities are jointly funded with other countries, with priorities and opportunities being shaped by mutual needs with the goal of building goodwill: "The Fulbright U.S. Student Program provides grants for individually designed study/research projects or for English Teaching Assistant programs. During their grants, Fulbrighters will meet, work, and learn from the people of the host country, sharing daily experiences. The program facilitates cultural exchange through direct interaction on an individual basis in the classroom, field, home, and in routine tasks, allowing the grantee to gain an appreciation of others' viewpoints and beliefs, the way they do things, and the way they think."[4] Students are expected to be flexible, open-minded, and receptive to other cultures and ideas so that they can return to the United States and pass these along in their professional careers.

There are many benefits to applying and receiving any type of Fulbright grant. These can be viewed both extrinsically and intrinsically. Extrinsically, Fulbright is an international achievement that adds to students' professional portfolios. Students also receive noncompetitive eligibility for federal employment.[5] Fulbright can lead to other opportunities and recognitions. According to the Fulbright website, alumni have achieved distinction in government, science, the arts, business, philanthropy, education, and athletics:

- 37 Fulbright alumni have served as heads of state or government.
- 59 Fulbright alumni from 14 countries have been awarded the Nobel Prize.
- 72 Fulbright alumni are MacArthur Foundation Fellows.
- 84 Fulbright alumni have received Pulitzer Prizes.[6]

Students who are awarded the U.S. Student Fulbright grant also bring recognition to their campuses and may encourage other like-minded students to apply.

The intrinsic rewards of the application process include self-discovery. Students must think about how they will serve as cultural ambassadors for the United States and what their plans are for civil engagement in the country they have chosen. Competitive Fulbright applicants need to develop a deep understanding of personal, academic, family, intellectual, and other past experiences and how these aspects of themselves tie strongly to their interest in the host country. All candidates, through the personal statement and other aspects of the application, will want to introduce themselves and convey their background, motivation, and the connection between Fulbright and their long-term future goals.

Students awarded the Fulbright have the opportunity for mutual exchange and to gain a unique perspective on other cultures. Fulbright is seeking those who wish to give back both in the United States and their host country. The Fulbright is a life-changing experience, and students may gain practical skills such as stronger foreign-language abilities, additional research or teaching experiences, and an extensive network of Fulbright alumni. The U.S. Student Fulbright also has various types of grants available that might need different approaches. Students can typically act as an English Teaching Assistant (ETA), conduct research, or study in the host country. Under the research area, students might be able to engage in a creative project such as dance or music or attend graduate school. Each type of Fulbright has its own set of criteria and thus its own set of challenges.

Students also have the opportunity to develop or increase diplomacy and leadership skills as a representative of the United States. Senator Fulbright addresses this key aspect of the program directly: "Our future is not in the stars but in our own minds and hearts. Creative leadership and liberal education, which in fact go together, are the first requirements for a hopeful future for humankind. Fostering these—leadership, learning, and empathy between cultures—was and remains the purpose of the international scholarship program."[7] To complete a Fulbright successfully, students must be adaptable and resilient, and for most the Fulbright experience leads to reflection about themselves and the global culture in which they live.

Understanding the Fulbright Process

The first step in building a strong Fulbright culture on a campus is to step back and seek as much information as possible, especially about the Fulbright U.S. Student Program itself. Gaining a deep understanding of the Fulbright and its processes is key to developing a strong campus culture. The best place to start reading is the Fulbright U.S. Student web page, which includes the FPA manual, an update for the current year, Fulbright events, PowerPoints to use with students, tutorials, posters, information about the campus review process, and instructions on how to observe a U.S. Student National Screening Committee (NSC).[8] NSC is the committee that selects students to become semifinalists. Many members of NAFA report that observing an NSC is most helpful in understanding what can make a student more competitive for Fulbright. The FPA manual is also detailed in giving suggestions for being successful in student recruitment and applications. There are nuances to Fulbright, however, and the NAFA listserv is a great place for discussing these in more detail. Fulbright offers trainings both in person and by webinars on the application, and FPAs can also request a visit from Fulbright using the "Request a Fulbright visit" within the FPA web page.

Ms. Lora Seery, senior program manager at the Institute of International Education (IIE), also recommends these additional steps:

- *"Know where to find 'quick' information.* Charts about ETA and graduate programs, stats, recorded webinars, and tutorials abound and can be extremely helpful to students as they are starting out in the process.
- *Spend some time exploring the website.* It is vast, but being familiar with it can help FPAs and future applicants identify information more quickly.
- *Understand that policies and processes change.* Continue to check the website for updates. Country descriptions and Fulbright Foreign Scholar Board (FFSB) regulations can and do change. Stay informed.
- *Demonstrate curiosity.* FPAs are never going to know everything there is to know about every country or award. When questions come in to an awards office, we hope that FPAs are modeling for applicants how to seek out appropriate resources.
- *Reach out with questions!* IIE is here to help. On the contact us page, FPAs and applicants can find phone numbers and email addresses for general and country specific inquiries. It is a big program, but we are here to help. Whenever there is a question that is not answered on the Web page, FPAs just need to pick up the phone."[9]

Learning about Campus Culture to Grow the Fulbright Program

The FPA does not have to work alone to create a strong Fulbright campus culture. Developing partnerships means more students receive information and opportunities. FPAs should conduct formal or informal assessments of the campus's strengths, weaknesses, challenges, and political climate as related to the Fulbright U.S. Student Program. The first step is to make a list of various departments as well as faculty and staff members who could assist in providing an overview of the campus.

Creating strong partnerships on campus can assist in the development of a Fulbright culture in many practical ways. Departments can hang Fulbright flyers and promote any Fulbright campus events. FPAs have more resources to directly encourage students to apply because these departments also have their own email listservs and hands-on events. For example, TRiO programs work directly with low-income and first-generation college students, who may need encouragement to consider themselves Fulbright material.

One successful recruitment tool that FPAs have used is emailing students individually to say they have been recognized as outstanding and referred to the FPA because of their many accomplishments. The start of this email might read "Dr. X has recommended you as a Fulbright candidate because of your recent STEM internship and accomplishments." Personal emails are often more effective than email blasts. Students involved in service learning also match the mentality of giving back that the Fulbright encompasses. Campus partnership with offices like Study Abroad reach students who are more likely to be interested in other cultures and worldviews. Students who conduct research or creative activities may find the Fulbright process less daunting and have critical thinking and creative talents. Honors colleges typically have a wide range of diverse students from different majors. No FPA should be an island but should connect to the academic and service areas of their campus. Offices that might offer assistance and advice include:

- Study abroad office and foreign language departments
- Honors college or merit scholarship center
- Undergraduate research center and/or STEM research centers
- Multicultural services
- Career services
- Programs like TRIO that work with low-income, first-generation students
- Faculty who previously were awarded Fulbrights or led study abroad programs

- Provost or leaders in academic affairs
- Service learning departments

Questions that might be helpful to ask as the program develops include:

- What are the strengths and challenges of the campus? What challenges do students face?
- What kind of data or metrics are administrators on campus concerned with?
- What are the general demographics on campus? How many minority, low-income, and first-generation students does the campus have? How many students work part-time and full-time?
- Which professors and departments have a reputation for being student centered?
- How do students learn about opportunities like internships and research opportunities?
- How many students study abroad? What types of study abroad?
- What is the culture on campus concerning studying abroad? If numbers are low, why is this so?
- What campus organizations might lend themselves to Fulbright?

By asking many open-ended questions in a nonjudgmental way, FPAs can understand better the strengths of their campus and the challenges ahead. Creating a strong Fulbright culture is a slow process, and the questions can also be asked over a longer period of time. Dr. Brian Souders, from the University of Maryland, Baltimore County, reported, "It is important to have manageable expectations during the learning curve of the Fulbright Program. Fulbright is a gigantic program, and advisors cannot expect to understand all of the pieces on the first, or even second, cycle. My favorite phrase that I repeat over and over again with students and faculty is, 'Well, it depends.' Fulbright is a program of 140+ different national programs, bound together only by the name Fulbright. Be patient. Don't be afraid to ask questions. The NAFA listserv is a tremendous asset; fellow NAFAns are a friendly, supportive group of colleagues who want to help!"[10] Understanding what stresses faculty and staff and also what motivates them to work with students can assist in building the campus Fulbright culture. Being sensitive to faculty deadlines and timetables can aid the FPA in timing requests and speaking engagements. Faculty appreciate recognition for their efforts, but what is valued might differ from campus to campus. Having one-on-one meetings with faculty is more effective in getting them to open up about what they like and do not like about offering assistance with other programs. Additionally, understanding campus retention issues can be helpful. What are the reasons students leave campus? Some information might be in the public domain through the department of institutional effectiveness or research, such as what percentage of students work full-time or part-time. FPAs need to understand why students might not want to apply for the Fulbright. FPAs also need to understand the political aspects and the top priorities for the campus. Building a strong network of faculty and staff champions is essential.

Using Technology to Aid in Cultural Development

When meeting with students, FPAs do not have to reinvent the wheel. The FPA toolbox on the website has forms and materials that can be used directly with students and faculty. If there is a current computer system that the campus uses to track and keep notes on students, the FPAs should consider using this first. One goal might be to track freshmen or sophomores who are good Fulbright candidates. Running GPA reports and sending emails to potential students about individual meetings or Fulbright campus events can help enhance the campus culture. Knowing which programs might "feed the flow" of Fulbright is key. Students who apply and show strong interest in these programs might be excellent candidates for Fulbright as they progress in their academic careers. These programs include: Boren Scholarships, Critical Language Scholarships, DAAD RISE, Benjamin A. Gilman Scholarships, Barry M. Goldwater Scholarships, MHIRTs (Minority Health and Health Disparities International Research Training Program), NSF REUs (National Science Foundation Research Experiences for Undergraduates), PPIA (Public Policy and International Affairs) opportunities, and Truman Scholarships.

Meeting with the campus information (IT) staff to determine the best method for creating recurring reports is recommended. Having standard reports to run to recruit students streamlines the Fulbright process.

Some examples of types of reports might be:

- Foreign-language majors with a 3.5 GPA or higher
- International studies, international business, and/or international relations majors again with a 3.5 GPA or higher
- First-generation and low-income students/Pell grants with 3.0 or higher
- Honors college students
- Students who studied abroad early in their academic careers

Additionally, FPAs should ask for a list of names and emails from the study abroad office and other offices like research centers with which they develop partnerships. FPAs also need to track and have a record-keeping system for meetings with potential students. A simple solution is to maintain an Excel file with names, emails, and countries of interest. There are systems available for purchase, and these vary widely among FPAs and universities. The main objective is to keep track of potential students and start developing long-term relationships with them.

FPAs also need to understand how social media is used on campus. Is the college Facebook page actually reviewed by students? What types of social media are most popular with staff, faculty, and students? Asking students directly during meetings can be an effective way to maintain and develop best communication practices.

Creating the Fulbright Plan of Action

Many FPAs have additional job responsibilities that might include teaching college classes, advising students, and recruitment or administrative job duties. The most effective way to promote the U.S. Student Fulbright is to make Fulbright connect to other areas of the FPA's position. Discuss Fulbright options in both formal and informal ways each time an opportunity arises. Promoting Fulbright should not exist in a vacuum, but needs to be part of an FPA's daily routine and connected to their other job responsibilities. FPAs who are teaching could add a fellowship or Fulbright section to their classes. Presenting Fulbright information at required workshops or orientation meetings for students is a great way to spread the word. Advisors can also expand the conversation by discussing

Critical Language, Gilman, Boren, and Freeman-Asia scholarships when discussing Fulbright. When attending faculty or staff meetings, advisors might ask to present Fulbright information for five to ten minutes. FPAs who are not faculty members should talk with key department chairs to see if such a presentation would be possible in their departments. All FPAs can hold drop-in sessions and provide food so students (and invited faculty) can visit at their convenience.

Once the FPA has assessed the campus culture, the next step is to create a plan of action that takes into account the campus's strengths and challenges. Creating informal and formal partnerships is important because the FPA alone cannot reach potential students. The first few years, an FPA should go "fishing" to find which departments will support the Fulbright program. Dr. Brian Souders notes, "Building a strong network of faculty and staff champions across campus is key, and it takes time. Do not expect instant results. But with time, patience, and a lot of friendly coffee and lunch meetings, advisors can build the network of supporters across campus who can lead to promising students."[11]

A typical Fulbright plan of action might include the following:

- A timeline with small steps of action
- Departments and faculty who might be most supportive of Fulbright
- Fulbright trainings that the FPA can attend
- GPA reports to run and when to contact students
- The creation of forms to collect student background information
- A selection of the social media outlets that best fit the campus culture
- A list of strategies for reaching students, which clubs or student events the FPA should attend
- Special recruitment events that the FPA can host like Fulbright Week, celebrating the start of the Fulbright competition
- A plan for the placement of highly visible posters, signs, and visual aids
- A celebration event for students who applied for Fulbright and the faculty who supported them
- A publicity plan that includes the news and public affairs department

Again, celebrating success is important and will increase faculty and student involvement in helping recruit additional students to the program. Acknowledging those who go through the application process, as well as those recommended as semifinalists or selected as finalists or alternates, is a great way to emphasize the importance of the process of applying—not only those who are successful.

Helping Students Be Successful

For many students, the Fulbright seems very overwhelming; first-generation, low-income students and those from underrepresented groups may not see themselves as Fulbright material. Brandy Simula gives a helpful overview of strategies for recruiting and advising for underrepresented students in her article "Belonging, Imposter Phenomenon, and Advising Students from Underrepresented Backgrounds," which is recommended reading for new FPAs.[12] For some students, a lack of a sense of belonging coupled with feeling like an imposter makes them less likely to apply for a Fulbright or other opportunities. Simula notes, "Because students from underrepresented backgrounds may be less likely to think of themselves as 'fellowship material' in comparison to students well represented in the academy, being intentional in the public image we craft for our offices, and in the visuals that we select to represent our offices, can play an important role in whether or not students from underrepresented backgrounds see our offices as ones that serve students like themselves."[13] These same students are likely to be modest in identifying their accomplishments, and advisors may need to take additional time to draw their leadership and success stories out as the student may see it as nothing special or worth mentioning.[14]

Breaking the Fulbright process into smaller and more manageable steps can assist these students in completing the Fulbright application. Ideally, students should gain insight into themselves just by applying for the Fulbright. Students can then use this process to apply for graduate school or other fellowships. Again, writing a personal statement is challenging, but can ultimately help them in other areas of their lives. The Fulbright application seems very basic to most professionals with just two essays, short answers, and three references, but being asked to weave a life narrative and explain long-term goals is new to many undergraduates who may have been focused on just getting their degree.

After advisors have attracted students to the Fulbright program (through emails, faculty outreach, drop-in sessions, or other means), they must devise a process that encourages students to persist. Having students watch Fulbright videos before appointments can be less overwhelming to them than asking them to review the entire Fulbright website. Conducting a personal interview during that first meeting, which includes many open-ended questions, will give a better sense of what the student might want to include in the application. Advisors can also make the application more digestible for students by dividing the application into smaller parts and setting very early internal deadlines that allow time for revisions.

Pointing students to links like "Culturegram" or similar websites provides easily accessible information about living conditions and cultural expectations in other countries to assist with essay writing and interview questions. Providing names of faculty with overseas research contacts or the opportunity to speak with former Fulbright students can also be extremely helpful. Sample applications of past successes to review within the fellowships office can help students think about how to frame their own stories. As the students begin requesting input, advisors should remember to give positive feedback first before launching into constructive suggestions.

The FPA may also want to address any personal and emotional concerns that the student might have about applying for the Fulbright. If a student is low-income, first-generation, or has not traveled widely, then the family might not support the student applying. Asking directly what the family is concerned about is recommended. FPAs should also ask students to describe in detail what they like or do not like about the country that they have chosen. Students who answer in vague terms or say "I just want to travel" need to be strongly encouraged to conduct more research, or the Fulbright interview may not go smoothly. Ideally, students should speak directly to former Fulbright recipients as well as faculty and students who have traveled to the country in which they are interested. FPAs want to offer encouragement and positive comments to students early and often, establishing a relationship where students feel free to discuss their concerns and fears about living in another country.

Students will have a better experience with the application, during the interview, and on their Fulbright if they have a deeper understanding of the cultural challenges ahead. Recommended reading for FPAs is Graham's "Student Ambassadors in the Age of Anti-Americanism," which discusses the need for students to understand anti-Americanism and the role of being a cultural ambassador. She notes that the term *ambassador* is often taken to mean "projecting an image: being courteous, continuing to study well, and exuding friendliness."[15] Students with such a shallow interpretation may be unprepared for their Fulbright experiences, and Graham recommends some specific strategies that they can use in preparation, including familiarizing themselves with the Constitution as "our approach to freedom of speech and religion (both frequently criticized as excessive) will be valuable tools in explaining the United States."[16] Students awarded a Fulbright need to be prepared to participate in deeper conversations with local citizens as part of their Fulbright community engagement.

In summary, open-minded and qualified students can benefit from applying to the Fulbright program regardless of the outcome. The first step in building a strong Fulbright culture on a campus is to step back and seek as much information as possible, especially about the Fulbright U.S. Student Program itself. The FPA does not have the sole responsibility of creating a strong Fulbright campus culture. Developing partnerships means more students receive information and opportunities. The goals of this article are to contribute to the base knowledge of new FPAs and generate discussion by experienced FPAs on how to create a plan of action for increasing Fulbright enthusiasm and participation among faculty, staff, and students on their campuses. Additional points for discussion are the challenges that underrepresented students may encounter in the application process and also in living in other countries, and FPAs will want to prepare strategies to assist their students and think critically about campus strengths, challenges, and culture, seeking input from colleagues and campus leaders, in order to build a culture that encourages a diverse community of students to embrace opportunities like the Fulbright Scholarship.

Notes

1. *Fulbright Advisor Manual* (2018), https://us.fulbrightonline.org.

2. Top Producers of U.S. Fulbright Students by Type of Institution, *The Chronicle of Higher Education* 59, no. 10 (2012): A18.

3. History of Fulbright U.S. Student Program (2019), https://us.fulbrightonline.org/about/history.

4. What is the Fulbright U.S. Student Program (2019), https://us.fulbrightonline.org/fulbright-us-student-program.

5. Noncompetitive Eligibility for Federal Employment, March 9, 2017, https://alumni.state.gov/highlight/noncompetitive-eligibility-federal -employment#.

6. Notable Fulbrighters (2019), https://eca.state.gov/fulbright/fulbright -alumni/notable-fulbrighters.

7. J. W. Fulbright. *Remarks by J. William Fulbright.* Speech presented at 30th Anniversary of the Fulbright Program, 1976.

8. *Fulbright Advisor Manual* (2018), https://us.fulbrightonline.org.

9. Lora Seery, Senior Program Manager, via email correspondence with Laura Clippard, January 2, 2019.

10. Brian Souders, Fulbright Program Advisor, via email correspondence with Laura Clippard, January 3, 2019.

11. Ibid.

12. B. Simula, "Belonging, Imposter Phenomenon, and Advising Students from Underrepresented Backgrounds," in *Roads Less Traveled and Other Perspectives on Nationally Competitive Scholarships*, eds. Suzanne McCray and Joanne Brzinski (Fayetteville: University of Arkansas Press, 2017), 121–34.

13. Ibid., 127.

14. Ibid., 121–34.

15. C. M. Graham, "Student Ambassadors in the Age of Anti-Americanism," in *Nationally Competitive Scholarships: Serving Students and the Public Good*, ed. Suzanne McCray (Fayetteville: University of Arkansas Press, 2007): 35–47.

16. Ibid.

10

NAFA Gone International
Supporting Global Applicants through the Fellowships Process

CHARLOTTE EVANS

Charlotte Evans was a fellowships advisor at Yale-NUS (National University of Singapore) College in Singapore for three years between 2015 and 2018, advising students from around the world who were applying to undergraduate and postgraduate funded opportunities. While at Yale-NUS, she organized the first study tour to China for the National Association of Fellowships Advisors. In her final year at the college, she received a fellowship from the Qatar Foundation's World Innovation Summit for Education (WISE) to develop innovations for refugee education, and through this role, looked at college access for refugees in Rwanda. Prior to joining Yale-NUS, she was a writing tutor and coordinator of the Deans' Service Scholars program at New York University (NYU), Shanghai. Evans graduated from NYU with a journalism and East Asian studies degree, with a Chinese language focus. She is currently pursuing a one-year master's degree at the Harvard Graduate School of Education in International Education Policy and wishes to explore ways in which scholarships and higher education can be affordable and accessible to all.

Fellowships advisors are privileged to have such a robust organization as the National Association of Fellowships Advisors (NAFA) to guide them in work supporting U.S. students applying for scholarships and fellowships. But what happens when a non-U.S. student enters a U.S. university's fellowships office, and how can advisors best guide these students to also thrive in the application process? The essay below focuses on my experiences working at Yale-NUS College in Singapore as a fellowships advisor providing support to students from over fifty countries. This is what I learned.

Background and Institutional Context

Before going into the details of navigating the cross-cultural differences and expectations around prestige, competition, and the value of postgraduate funded opportunities for U.S. and non-U.S. students, it is important to set the stage of why Yale-NUS (National University of Singapore) exists, as it is the institution from which these insights are drawn. Yale-NUS welcomed its inaugural cohort of students to Singapore in June 2013.[1] In its mission statement, Yale-NUS College says that it "aims to redefine liberal arts and science education for a complex, interconnected world" and would do so by borrowing fundamental elements of the American liberal arts education for its new curriculum.[2] Thanks to generous funding from the Singaporean government, who provided Tuition Grant Schemes for students, tuition fees were reduced substantially for undergraduate students who opted into this scheme.[3]

Former Yale president Richard Levin and current president Peter Salovey wrote a joint memo in 2010 noting that the college was being established in Singapore to provide students an education that would allow them "to address problems for which there are no easy solutions."[4] Through content specialization provided by a diverse offering of majors, and the Centre for International and Professional Experience (CIPE) office where I worked as a fellowships advisor, students were explicitly trained to navigate conversations on diversity and apply this to life outside of the classroom and in the workforce.[5] The institution brought together students from around the world, with a breakdown of 60 percent Singaporean and 40 percent international students,[6] to study and live together for four years. As a fellowships advisor, I had the privilege to work with students from a wide range of backgrounds and saw the pivotal role of an accessible higher education model in shaping students' lives for the better. I advised students from Colombia, Laos, New Zealand, Singapore, Spain, Sweden, and many other places around the globe. They each had individual aspirations, country-defined ideals of strong leadership, and plans to settle in disparate locations after graduation.

When I first stepped into this role, I reflected upon how I could create a singular platform that would accommodate the multitude of individual needs from this blend of students. First, our office needed to assess if there were any preconceived understandings of this word *fellowships* within our campus community. Our first batch of graduates completed their degree in May 2017, which meant that when I began fellowships advising in 2015, there was no previous alumni cohort of award recipients to provide visibility of what a fellowship was and the impact an award might have on the lives and academic trajectory of students after Yale-NUS. Not only that, but if students Google "Singapore fellowships" to try to crack the code on their own, they will find some of the top responses are linked to medical school study at Singapore's National University Hospital and to several religious organizations that provide Christian fellowship in the country. The takeaway was that *global fellowships* were a foreign land.

While much changed with regard to visibility over the three years of my work at Yale-NUS, the main roadblock I observed in advising international students stemmed from limited visibility of these awards, simply because of ineligibility issues. For example, there was no Rhodes Scholar funding for Singaporean nationals between 2006 and its reinstatement in 2018. This meant that the last time Singapore had a Rhodes Scholar before it was reinstated, its first batch of graduating seniors were enrolling in first grade.[7] Not only that, but the Singapore government's offering of Public Service Commission Scholarships[8] that link students to a ministry and bond a student to a work placement postgraduation in exchange for a funded postgraduate degree overseas in a related field of study means that Singaporeans have several robust funding structures already at home. The bond structure, which affords students the opportunity to study abroad with a commitment to work in Singapore upon completion of their program for a certain tenure of years, is typically around three years, but can be more depending on the full cost of the degree.[9] Given the visibility of these nationally funded opportunities, our office was tasked to

Figure 10.1. Open Doors Report 2016

INTERNATIONAL STUDENTS IN THE U.S. 1953/54 - 2015/16

In 2015/16 there was **an increase of 7%** over the prior year in the number of international students in the U.S.

Open Doors is conducted by the Institute of International Education with the support of the Bureau of Educational and Cultural Affairs of the U.S. Department of State. Online at www.iie.org/opendoors

open**doors**

prompt students to see the possibility of a second pathway for funded study through global fellowship opportunities that reached beyond the regional bounds of Southeast Asia.

Reflecting these findings back to the larger fellowships advisor community, it may be that international students at U.S. campuses, who might be strong candidates for a global fellowship, need an additional nudge to look beyond their national offerings if they hail from a country that has similar funding structures as Singapore for postgraduate education. Each year, the Institute for International Education provides research through their Open Doors report that shows the influx of international students entering into the United States. As shown in Figure 10.1,[10] there was an increase of 7 percent in 2015 to 2016 of international students in the United States. While the recent strength of the U.S. dollar and student visa reform are associated with the decrease in the two most recent years of international students studying in the United States,[11] there are still large percentages of non-U.S. students arriving on U.S. campuses each year. Considering the growing number of international students who are choosing to pursue their studies at campuses in the United States, fellowships advisors may be asked by their senior leadership to understand this globalized context for the sake of best serving their full student population.

Figure 10.2. Open Doors Report 2016

TOP TEN PLACES OF ORIGIN OF INTERNATIONAL STUDENTS

60% of international students
come from China, India, Saudi Arabia, and South Korea.

Open Doors is conducted by the Institute of International Education
with the support of the Bureau of Educational and Cultural Affairs
of the U.S. Department of State. Online at www.iie.org/opendoors

open**doors**®

Is it realistic to expect every fellowships advisor to know the nuances of eligibility and local funding structures for every nationality of student that comes through the door? Absolutely not. So how can professional scholarship advisors make some strategic decisions to support the highest percentage of U.S. and international students on their own campuses? Sixty percent of the identified international students from IIE's Open Doors report come from China, India, Saudi Arabia, and South Korea.[12] While each campus may deviate in its percentage breakdown of nationalities, admissions offices may be able to provide nationality percentages to fellowships advisors who can correlate the campus information with the broader IIE data. For example, in my work in Singapore, I advised a majority of students from Southeast Asia and China on fellowships. However, in a U.S. office for a university that does targeted outreach in other parts of the world, there might be a wholly different demographic. Worthy to note in the IIE Open Doors country-specific data in Figure 10.2 is that four countries are responsible for 60 percent of international students in the United States studying in 2015–2016, with 32 percent coming from China and 16 percent from India. If a fellowships advisor were to make a first foray into supporting international students intentionally and doing research to understand the preexisting scholarships landscape on two specific countries, the data indicate the best bet is to look at China and India first.

Fortunately, the globalization movement is taking hold with fellowships providers as well, which allows NAFA advisors to direct students to a myriad of offerings for which they are eligible. For example, the Rhodes Scholarship has increased partnerships with eligibility in Israel, Jordan, Lebanon, Malaysia, Palestine, Syria, the UAE, West Africa, and Singapore and announced their global scholarship placement as well.[13] Additionally, there are newer fellowships that are charging ahead with global eligibility from the start through newly defined, internationally inclusive admissions policies. Two notable examples of scholarships without nationality requirements include Schwarzman Scholars, with its first class in 2016 at Tsinghua University, and the Knight-Hennessy Scholarship, which welcomed its first class this year in fall 2018 to Stanford University.

However, with this newer trend, fellowships advisors may feel a growing additional pressure from senior leadership on campus to start identifying non-U.S. students to apply for these globally open opportunities. This can be a daunting process. Below are three areas where I adapted my advising practice to meet students on their own cultural turf. While I hope these takeaways are useful, I wish to preface the following text with a note that these concepts were crafted primarily through practice and should be interpreted as such.

The Culture of Leadership

In a 2017 CNBC special called "Schwarzman Scholars Program: A $500 Million Scholarship That May Someday Change the World," two students discussed their own understandings of their personal leadership while in the master's program in ways that reveal cultural differences. During the video, several of the selected American students discuss the welcome from Steven Schwarzman and their decision to be a part of a program that prides itself on creating global leaders in the twenty-first century. The video shows a female scholar from the United States explaining that Schwarzman's lecture telling the selected students that they are the next global leaders "lit a fire under me." The video then shows another U.S. male student, who tells the film crew with a smile, that "I've always wanted to be President of the United States."[14] Part of the multimedia presentation done by CNBC on this scholarship program had additional videos talking about the cultural differences associated with leadership. In the second segment, "A Clash of Cultures When It Comes to Leadership," we hear from a Chinese student who narrates one of the key differences in his perception on leadership during his schooling. "You do not talk about leadership until you are more established or until you are older," the Chinese national selected for the program says. "I think it is definitely part of a humble and modest culture that traditional Chinese history values. When talking to my Chinese friends, I do feel a little bit embarrassed when I tell people, 'Hey, this program is all about building future young leaders.'"[15] The key words of *humility, modesty,* and *embarrassment* described by this Chinese student in relation to a lack of desirability to discuss his own leadership stood out here, in juxtaposition to the claims from the American student who aspired to be President of the United States.

When working with global student leaders who wished to pursue roles of leadership in their profession down the road, I found it helpful to have a priming conversation about the types and locations of leadership they envisioned in their future. Within the Yale-NUS context, our students often wanted to be policy makers, thought leaders, and activists. I saw that many of our fellowships applicants came from the Asian-Pacific area (APAC) primarily and wanted to stay in APAC for the long run. This meant that on our campus, the United States did not enter onto the table of possibilities in a majority of the conversations of the students' global narratives. More reluctant students on my campus were motivated through a scaffolded advising session where geographic needs over their own leadership style provided a platform for more open discourse around their candidacy for an opportunity. We examined the facts of their prior leadership experience rather than the emotions around the weight of the meaning of "being a leader." As an advisor, I researched trending topics or movements in APAC that needed up-and-coming leaders to guide the way and solve long-term problems, whether it be STEM research financing in India, small-state diplomacy in Asia Pacific, or environmental air quality in China. By being well versed in these issues, I could then ask students how specific areas of their previous experience aligned with the current demands in these professions. Our conversations would then be structured around future growth of the field's change rather than the student's singular leadership vision.

These patterns on my Singaporean campus often looked at key market issues in India and China. However, this might not be the geographic target area for international students in the U.S. academic scene who aspire to remain in the U.S. postgraduation. Students may confide in other offices around campus about their true postgraduation goals, so a fellowships advisor who cultivates relationships with admissions, international student offices, and career services to foster strong collaborations will garner practical information about their students in the pre-advising stage. The Yale-NUS office involved senior leadership at the college to identify students who have thrived at the all-campus level, facilitated workshops through student life to talk about leadership with student organization leaders during their sophomore year, and identified key faculty players and mentors who encouraged students to apply and tackle these ambitious leadership goals. Through this collaborative spirit, we saw more international students attending information sessions and completing our institutional endorsement application process.

Leadership in Relation to Gender

How did gender factor into my perception of students' pursuit of programs that emphasized leadership in non-U.S. contexts? Our office noted in our first year of applications that many of our highly qualified Southeast Asian female applicants were exceptional information gatherers during the information sessions and would show up for initial advising appointments. When it came time to actually apply to these opportunities, however, suddenly then felt they were "not a good fit" or that it was not the "right time" for them to apply. We noticed a heavy skew of these rationales from our female applicants over our male applicants. From year one to year two of our advising practice, our continued efforts to build out personalized mentorship for students from faculty, and particularly making known nominations from female faculty to female students, prompted a percentage increase in retention of female applicants from initial advising appointments to submission of applications. This gendered participation issue spanned all cultural backgrounds on our campus, but by recognizing the intersection of gender and cultural norms around leadership, our office was able to serve female students from Asia more effectively.

Individual vs. Collective Identities

One year, I worked with a bright Chinese-Singaporean student who conducted phenomenal lab-based research, under the tutelage of a world-class professor. And yet, when writing of these experiences on a resume and discussing them with an interview panel for a fellowship, he deferred to the expertise of the faculty research lead and reduced the significant impact he as a student had on the direction of the research.

Alberto Melucci's research from 1995 on the collective identity might provide some clues as to why this happened. Melucci wrote, "The tendency and need to stabilize one's identity and to give it a permanent form create a tension between the results of the process, which are crystallized in more or less permanent structures, in more or less stable definitions of identity, and the process itself, which is concealed behind those forms."[16] This student might have felt concealed in Melucci's described process, while the professor, in the student's eye, was a more "permanent structure." In a 2018 article about Chinese international students' sense of connectedness,[17] Chun Cao and colleagues referenced sentiments of perceived prejudice in relation to social connectedness and social support for Chinese international students based in France at the time of the study. Wheeler, Reis, and Bond also discussed the role of collectivism for Hong Kong students, who relied more heavily on groups for tasks over their university student counterparts in the United States.[18] Referencing back to the Chinese-Singaporean student researcher, under Cao and Wheeler's frameworks of collectivism, this student promoted the work of the professor, who is esteemed and established, over his own contributions in the lab during his time there for the sake of social harmony. Anecdotally, this awareness around harmony-seeking for collectivism played out in my office in a very specific way, when I asked many of the students from Eastern cultures to replace "we" with "I" in their personal statements. By recognizing their individual prior academic and professional efforts in writing, students from collectivist backgrounds can stand on equal footing in their prose with students who might innately choose to describe their own personal victories with singularity.

Next, we reframed the tension between highlighting individual academic excellence and the hesitation to self-promote by removing the notion of a connection between excellence with self-promotion in how we advised. We found that by highlighting the placement of content-specific stakeholders and their roles in fitting into the larger collective mentality, students found comfort in promoting their own role within the context of broader goals. It drew attention to the mission at large, which allowed students to talk about themselves in a more comfortable way. In these conversations, I encouraged students to "think of themselves as a primary text," which also removed any sort of uncomfortable diary-like chattiness around their experience and resulted in students boiling down their expertise to the facts—they surrounded themselves with evidence about their experience rather than resting on subjective attestations of leadership they felt uncomfortable displaying in a public essay. Alberto Melucci spoke once more about this subject when he wrote later, "Collective identity therefore defines the capacity for autonomous action, a differentiation of the actor from others while continuing to be itself."[19]

When we reframed the story of the Singaporean student in the lab who had previously refused to speak on his work in authentic ways by diminishing his role to simple lab tasks, we saw a sudden capacity to contextualize the work in a meaningful way that promoted his own intellectual strength in a broader conversation. The student saw that his research was in fact critical for the larger body of knowledge. His audience was then able to deduce his role as a pivotal stakeholder in the broader academic narrative of that specific lab's research.

Effecting Change on a Student's Own Terms

Working with international students provided an exciting new window of learning for advisors and a chance to navigate interesting conversations around global diversity with students. While cultivating one's own cross-cultural intuition can be of great use in our advising practice, the role of the advisor is also to set realistic knowledge expectations with the students they support. Expanded global eligibility for many awards allows students to explore opportunities worldwide. To make the advising process efficient with students from so many nationalities, I asked my students to first write down on their own: 1) a few scholarships of interest that were open and eligible to their nationality, 2) where they wished to reside in the future, 3) any current constraints based on undergraduate scholarships provided by their home country that might have a bond or work requirement postgraduation, and 4) how they will infuse their undergraduate education in Singapore alongside their national upbringing to effect change in the best way they know how going forward. Once a student identified those four aspects of their future planning, our conversation was much more effective and streamlined.

Once a student has situated their ambitions for future study region-ally, it is then important to develop a contextually specific regional voice for their applications. Students must be aware of their audience, their geo-graphic understanding, and value placement on social change, so that they can write and speak effectively to a broad or unknown array of panelists making selection decisions. A prime example that took place at our office at Yale-NUS was with the Young Southeast Asian Leadership Initiative (YSEALI).[20] This U.S. State Department–funded exchange program, developed during President Obama's administration, was for undergrad-uates and young professionals from the Association of Southeast Asian Nations (ASEAN) to study for a semester in the United States on topics of civic engagement, environmentalism, and entrepreneurship. Many of my Singaporean students decided to apply for this opportunity. Given the themes of social entrepreneurship and how that mapped onto the broader discourse around Singaporean civic society, the advising process on the role of narrative voice in creating a compelling and agile argument for a variety of political audiences was an interesting process. The most effective students recognized both the positive growth to date in Singapore's youth-ful fifty years as a nation (at the time of writing their statements), which has made significant progress in many other arenas while also showing the alignment with the goals of YSEALI to a U.S. audience to promote further provocative civic engagement. There is no black-and-white answer for writing and navigating this balance in the application process. Students who showed an ability to handle bilateral diplomacy in their responses that catered to both Singaporean and U.S. political audiences stood out.

Navigating these difficult diplomatic ideas with grace in an applica-tion essay may be challenging for students who worry about the cultural expectations of saving face. Wenshan Jia writes in the book *The Remaking of the Chinese Character and Identity in the 21st Century: The Chinese Face Practices*: "In reconstructing Chinese personhood, lian/mian and harmony should be treated as tools to maximize individual happiness while respect-ing the rights of others to it."[21] Note the emphasis on the word *harmony* in this quotation. Under Jia's premise of balancing personal happiness while maintaining harmony through saving face (i.e., removing oneself from potentially divisive situations that cause embarrassment), students may avoid leaning into application essays or statements of purpose that incite disruptive solutions in their academic field of interest. Jia goes on to explain this focus further, "The excessive emphasis on harmony originates from Confucianism, which regards differences, uncertainty, and change as sources of disorder and hence to be avoided at all costs. This 'harmony' is actually a euphemism for homogeneity and conformity."[22] For the 34 percent of Chinese students studying overseas in the United States, this might be particularly true. To best advise those applicants, advisors must understand the "lian mian," or saving face, culture and how it may be the deciding factor for students wishing to pursue graduate research in subjects resting in more contentious geopolitical situations.

Our role as fellowships advisors may not then be to change students' perceptions of how to promote change, but rather to direct them to geographic scholarship opportunities where a vision alignment for reform processes is present. Starting these conversations early with students is important to first understand how they view the geopolitical climate where they will eventually settle in and study, as this will influence how they approach tough problem-solving situations in their professional and academic future. Advisors can encourage and prompt students to understand the idea of a stakeholder in creating reform, to choose when they will lean into nonconformity, and when they will step back into broader preexisting government frameworks, and to consider the groundwork for working within the structure to push forward any sort of positive social change.

Building Out an International Advising Practice

Below are some suggestions to help fellowships advisors navigate these cultural differences and expectations around prestige so that their global applicants can thrive during the advising process. These tangible steps streamlined processes in my office and may transfer beyond the Singapore context to fellowships offices across the United States.

Develop a pre-advising questionnaire. A systematic approach for identifying eligibility through a pre-advising form will expedite timelines around initial advising. The Yale-NUS office used one, which can also be found on its fellowships website. A form of this nature will encourage students to identify areas of academic and research interest, direct students to the fellowships listings website, and ask them to determine five or six options that will fund that academic interest. Notably, this form helped recalibrate expectations of access for our non-U.S. students.

Many U.S. State Department–funded opportunities are only open to U.S. citizens, which seemed to make some of my students feel that the landscape of funding was falsely distorted toward one nationality. This often prompted a sense of "unfairness" felt by non-U.S. students. Having a pre-advising questionnaire allowed students to identify several awards for which they qualify as international students. Advisors can then focus on positive, tangible prospects and open awards with students to keep momentum going in the application process.

Get to know country eligibility for major awards. The Yale-NUS Fellowships page has an array of fellowships offered to non-U.S. students that also lists the country eligibility for each opportunity.[23]

Explore other non–U.S. government funding models. The "U.S. to the rest of the world" bilateral relations are only a sliver of the full bilateral possibilities for academic exchange. There are many other bilateral exchange agreements around education. For fellowships offices wishing to explore ways to share this information with their international students, note that there are many resources available to support those endeavors. Other state departments and ministries of education are investing in education exchange. While a qualified international student will not be eligible for the Gilman or Pickering, there may be a government-specific opportunity in their own country for which they will qualify. In Australia, the government has provided a robust listing and database, for example, for opportunities to study both in Australia and for its citizens to continue study abroad through government scholarships.[24]

Many of the global Fulbright partners housed in the U.S. embassies overseas provide additional funding possibilities, as the $35,000 Fulbright grant for non-U.S. students to study in the United States may not cover more than one of the two years of study for some postgraduate opportunities. This is true for many of the large Fulbright offices around the globe, which often house their information on their U.S. embassy websites or will send these documents to advisors upon email request. These contacts can be found on the U.S. embassy sites[25] rather than through IIE or the general U.S. Student Fulbright portal.

Finally, advisors should visit the national university websites of the key countries that are represented on their university campuses. More online resources through these national universities are available about regional scholarship opportunities. The National University of Singapore has ample postings on postgraduate funding opportunities for its own students.[26]

Streamline the advising process. By encouraging international students to identify what they want to study and where they want to go geographically for their studies before they can book an advising appointment, advisors can start crowdsourcing possible awards to make scheduled meetings as efficient as possible. Time will be well spent mapping out possibilities and limitations with a student before talking about specific awards. For example, a student with a government-bonded scholarship from Singapore that mandates they return to their country to "work off the bond" after graduation from their U.S. bachelor's institution may wish to consider scholarship offerings three years from now but should not be discussing institutional endorsements for this upcoming year with an advisor.

Conclusion

The resources and anecdotes presented here may help in thinking about ways to better support international students globally, but many of these stories are tied specifically to the Yale-NUS and Singapore context. Advisors must evaluate how best to serve international students on their own campuses. Sharing news and resources through collaborations with other offices, such as admissions and international student support services, might attract more non-U.S. students to book their first advising meeting at a fellowships office.

Once these students arrive, management of student expectations will be key, by establishing that a realistic outcome for an advisor is to have in-depth understanding of four or five of the most represented countries on campus and then to build strategies and pathways for students from other international backgrounds to navigate the fellowships eligibility and alignment process independently. Placing the responsibility back onto the student to navigate the scholarships eligibility identification process will allow for a successful increase in support of students and a well-resourced, and rested, fellowships advisor who can work with students from all nationalities to offer catered advice for each award and process.

Notes

1. Yale-NUS College, "Milestones." (2019), https://www.yale-nus.edu.sg /about/milestones.

2. Yale-NUS College, "Vision and Mission." (2019), https://www.yale-nus .edu.sg/about/vision-and-mission

3. Yale-NUS College, "Financial Matters." (2019), https://admissions.yale -nus.edu.sg/financial-matters

4. Richard Levin and Peter Salovey, "Prospectus for a Liberal Arts College in Singapore," September 12, 2010, https://web.archive.org/web /20131212093625/http://communications.yale.edu/sites/default/files/YNC -Prospectus-2010-09.pdf.

5. Yale-NUS College, "About CIPE." (2019). https://cipe.yale-nus.edu.sg /about.

6. Yale-NUS College, "Yale-NUS College Fact Sheet," December, 2018, https://www.yale-nus.edu.sg/about/yale-nus-fact-sheet/.

7. Rhodes Trust, "Reinstatement of the Rhodes Scholarship for Singapore, in Partnership with APS Asset Management," January 29, 2018, https://www .rhodeshouse.ox.ac.uk/news-events/latest-news/news/2018/january /reinstatement-of-the-rhodes-scholarship-for-singapore-in-partnership-with-aps -asset-management.

8. Public Service Commission Singapore, "PSC Scholarships," July 17, 2017, https://www.psc.gov.sg/Scholarships/psc-scholarships.

9. Pak Tee Ng, "The Global War for Talent: Responses and Challenges in the Singapore Higher Education System," *Journal of Higher Education Policy and Management* 35, no. 3 (June 14, 2013): 280–92. https://doi.org/10.1080 /1360080X.2013.786859.

10. Institute of International Education, "Top 25 Places of Origin of International Students, 2015/2016–2016/2017." (2017). *Open Doors Report on International Educational Exchange*, https://www.iie.org/opendoors.

11. Yeganeh Torbati, "Fewer Foreign Students Coming to United States for Second Year in Row: Survey," *Reuters*, November 13, 2018, https://www.reuters .com/article/us-usa-immigration-students/fewer-foreign-students-coming-to -united-states-for-second-year-in-row-survey-idUSKCN1NI0EN.

12. Institute of International Education, "Top 25 Places of Origin."

13. Rhodes Trust, "List of Rhodes Scholarship Countries." (2018), https:// www.rhodeshouse.ox.ac.uk/scholarships/list-of-rhodes-scholarship-countries.

14. CNBC, "Schwarzman Scholars Program, a $500 Million Scholarship

That May Someday Change the World," June 23, 2017, https://www.youtube
.com/watch?v=GvstceFP4q8&t=0m59s.

15. CNBC, "A Clash of Cultures When It Comes to Leadership," June 26,
2017, https://www.cnbc.com/video/2017/06/26/a-clash-of-cultures-when-it
-comes-to-leadership.html.

16. Alberto Melucci, "The Process of Collective Identity," *Social Movements
and Cultures*, November 5, 2013, 46, https://www.taylorfrancis.com/books
/9781134224029/chapters/10.4324%2F9781315072562-8.

17. Chun Cao, Qian Meng, and Liang Shang, "How Can Chinese Interna-
tional Students' Host-National Contact Contribute to Social Connectedness,
Social Support, and Reduced Prejudice in the Mainstream Society? Testing a
Moderated Mediation Model," *International Journal of Intercultural Relations* 63
(March 2018). https://www.sciencedirect.com/science/article/abs/pii
/S014717671730130X.

18. Ladd Wheeler, Harry T. Reis, and Michael Bond, "Collectivism-
Individualism in Everyday Social Life: The Middle Kingdom and the Melting
Pot," *Journal of Personality and Social Psychology* 51, no. 1 (July 1989): 79–86.
https://psycnet.apa.org/doiLanding?doi=10.1037%2F0022-3514.57.1.79

19. Melucci, "The Process of Collective Identity," 47.

20. U.S. Mission to ASEAN, "Young Southeast Asian Leaders Initiative,"
https://asean.usmission.gov/yseali.

21. Wenshan Jia, *The Remaking of the Chinese Character and Identity in the
21st Century: The Chinese Face Practices* (Westport, CT: Ablex, 2001), 13.

22. Ibid.

23. Yale-NUS College, Browse Fellowships. (2019), https://cipe.yale-nus.edu
.sg/leadership-development/fellowships/browse-fellowships.

24. Australian Government, Scholarships to Study in Australia, https://www
.studyinaustralia.gov.au/english/australian-education/scholarships.

25. Fulbright Program for Foreign Students, Applicants, https://foreign
.fulbrightonline.org/applicants.

26. National University of Singapore, Scholarships for Current NUS Undergraduates. http://www.nus.edu.sg/oam/scholarships/current-nus
-undergraduates.

Part IV

On the Profession

11

NAFA Survey of the Profession 2019

The *NAFA Survey of the Profession* is conducted biennially. The 2019 survey was conducted in the spring of 2019 with 269 responses submitted overall, a 44 percent increase in participation from the previous year. Not all respondents answered every question. The percentages included are computed based on number of completed responses. Fellowships advisors and program directors have found this information useful as they start new offices or programs, make resource requests, prepare grants, create strategic plans, or draft annual reviews. New questions have been added this year and are indicated below with an (*). As always, the results are descriptive and are not intended for other forms of analysis or for research purposes.

Survey creation, distribution, and collection were conducted by two members from the NAFA Communications Committee: Lauren Tuckley, Chair, from Georgetown University, and Brian Davidson from Claremont McKenna College, with assistance from Brad Lutes, University of Arkansas.

Gender

Respondents indicated the gender identity with which they most identify.

Male	22.0%
Female	77.2%
Gender variant/Non-conforming	0.4%
No response	0.4%

Age

Respondents indicated their current age range.

Under 25	1.5%
26–30	5.6%
31–40	31.8%
41–50	32.6%
51–60	18.0%
Over 60	10.5%

Race

Respondents indicated whether they were American Indian or Alaskan Native, Asian or Pacific Islander, black or African American, Hispanic or Latino, white, or other.

American Indian or Alaskan Native	0.0%
Asian or Pacific Islander	3.3%
Black or African American	3.7%
Hispanic/Latino	2.6%
Other	1.1%
White	89.4%

Salary

Respondents indicated their annual salary range in their current positions.

Less than $50,000	15.8%
$50,000–$59,999	16.1%
$60,000–$69,999	21.7%
$70,000–$79,999	17.3%
$80,000–$99,999	17.3%
$100,000 or more	11.8%

Education Level

Respondents indicated the highest level of education that they have obtained.

Bachelor's or master's degree	46.1%
Doctorate or terminal professional degree (JD, MD, MBA, etc.)	53.9%

Title

Respondents indicated their job titles.

Director	37.3%
Assistant/Associate Director	22.0%
Coordinator	10.5%
Dean or Assistant/Associate Dean	8.6%
Other	21.6%

(The most common *Other* response was Advisor [9.0%].)

Faculty

Respondents indicated whether they currently hold a faculty position.

Yes	24.2%
No	75.8%

Employment with Current Institution

Respondents reported the number of years they have been employed at their current college or university.

0–3 years	25.1%
4–6 years	19.9%
7–10 years	17.6%
11–15 years	15.4%
More than 15 years	22.1%

Employment in Current Position

Respondents reported the number of years they have been employed in their current position as a fellowships advisor.

0–3 years	47.2%
4–6 years	24.9%
7–10 years	13.6%
More than 10 years	14.3%

Fellowships Advising Experience

Respondents reported the total number of years they have worked with fellowships activities.

0–3 years	33.0%
4–6 years	22.1%
7–10 years	19.1%
11–15 years	15.0%
More than 15 years	10.9%

Fellowships Advising Appointment

Respondents indicated whether their position is dedicated to full-time fellowships advising.

Full time	30.7%
Part time	69.3%

Fellowships Advising Appointment If Less Than Full Time

Respondents with a part-time fellowships advising appointment indicated what percentage of their employment is attributed to work with fellowships advising.

Less than 20% of time	22.7%
20%–39% of time	28.6%
40%–59% of time	24.4%
60%–79% of time	14.3%
80% of time or more	10.1%

Daily Fellowships Workload

Respondents indicated how many hours per day they spend on fellowships activities.

Less than 2 hours	13.6%
2–3 hours	15.5%
4–5 hours	18.1%
6–7 hours	19.3%
8–9 hours	26.8%
10 or more hours	6.8%

Summer Hours

Respondents indicated whether they have a nine-month base salary and, if so, how many hours per week during the summer they devote to fellowship-related duties.

5 hours or less	5.3%
6–10 hours	3.3%
11–20 hours	3.3%
21 or more hours	2.0%
12-month appointment	86.2%

Additional Duties

Respondents indicated their job duties other than fellowships advising.

Teaching	41.4%
Other	36.4%
Academic advising	30.5%
Honors programming	29.6%
Undergraduate research	28.6%
Administer university-based merit awards	27.7%
Research	22.3%
Career/Pre-professional advising	19.6%
Study abroad/International	15.0%
Service learning/Community outreach	6.8%

(The majority of the *Other* responses involve some type of administrative/supervisory/coordinating role.)

Career in Fellowships Advising

Respondents indicated whether they plan to remain in fellowships advising as a career.

Yes	41.3%
No	13.1%
Not sure	45.6%

Career Path

Respondents indicated their intended career paths.

Fellowships advising	44.7%
University administration outside fellowships	30.2%
Faculty	19.2%
Employment outside academia	6.0%

Type of Institution—Public or Private

Respondents indicated the nature of their institutions.

Public	49.4%
Private	50.6%

Type of Institution—Carnegie Classification

Respondents indicated the nature of their institutions.

Research or Doctoral-granting University	60.0%
Master's colleges and universities	18.1%
Baccalaureate colleges	21.5%
Other	0.4%

Size of College or University

Respondents indicated the number of undergraduate students currently enrolled at their institutions.

Fewer than 3,000	20.8%
3,001–9,000 students	30.9%
9,001–20,000 students	21.9%
20,001 or more students	26.4%

Student Populations Served

Respondents indicated all populations to which fellowships services are available.

Undergraduates	95.1%
Graduate Students	56.6%
Professional Students	24.2%
Alumni	75.5%
Students at regional/satellite campuses	11.3%

Nature of Office

Respondents indicated if their institutions have an office dedicated to fellowships advising, or if fellowships advising is part of the activities of a larger office.

Dedicated fellowships advising office	46.5%
Fellowships advising activities are part of larger office	42.3%
Other	11.2%

(Most common *Other* response was "No office.")

Office Makeup and Composition*

Respondents indicated the makeup and composition of their office.

One-person stand-alone office dedicated primarily to fellowships	23.2%
Multi-person office dedicated primarily to fellowships	25.5%
Office dedicated primarily to other roles	30.8%
No specific office	6.1%
Other	14.5%

(No trend was discernible for *Other*.)

History of Advising

Respondents indicated for how many years dedicated fellowships advising has existed at their institutions.

0–3 years	14.6%
4–6 years	15.8%
7–10 years	24.1%
11–15 years	17.0%
More than 15 years	28.5%

Location of Advising

Respondents indicated where fellowships advising is organizationally housed at their institutions.

Office of the Provost/VP for Academic Affairs	35.1%
Honors program	24.2%
Office of the Dean/Associate Dean	14.0%
Career/professional services	5.3%
Other	21.5%

(No trend was discernible for *Other*.)

Budget

Respondents indicated the operating budget (excluding salaries) for their fellowships office or activities.

Less than $1,000	25.4%
$1,001–$3,000	13.6%
$3,001–$6,000	13.6%
$6,001–$9,000	11.4%
$9,001–$15,000	20.8%
More than $15,000	15.3%

Staff Positions*

Respondents indicated the number of FTE staff positions, including respondents, devoted specifically to fellowships advising in each of the categories Faculty, Staff, Graduate Students, Undergraduate Students.

Faculty

None	64.7%
Less than 1	25.7%
Between 1 and 2	7.3%
More than 2	2.3%

Staff

None	25.0%
Less than 1	20.4%
Between 1 and 2	30.0%
More than 2	24.6%

Graduate Students

None	75.6%
Less than 1	15.2%
Between 1 and 2	6.1%
More than 2	3.0%

Undergraduate Students

None	87.6%
Less than 1	6.2%
Between 1 and 2	4.7%
More than 2	1.6%

Support Staff Positions*

Respondents indicated the number of FTE staff positions employed to support fellowships advising.

Faculty

None	92.1%
Less than 1	4.5%
Between 1 and 2	1.7%
More than 2	1.7%

Staff

None	53.5%
Less than 1	28.6%
Between 1 and 2	13.2%
More than 2	4.7%

Graduate Students

None	86.7%
Less than 1	8.8%
Between 1 and 2	3.3%
More than 2	1.1%

Undergraduate Students

None	81.0%
Less than 1	13.8%
Between 1 and 2	1.1%
More than 2	4.2%

Funding for Professional Development

Respondents indicated whether they receive funds for professional development related to fellowships advising.

Yes	94.0%
No	6.0%

Funding for Student Travel

Respondents indicated whether their institutions provide travel funds to students who have been invited for fellowship interviews.

Yes	68.9%
No	31.1%

Strategic Goals

Respondents indicated whether they have strategic goals for their fellowships activities.

Yes	57.2%
No	18.3%
Not yet but plan to develop some	24.5%

Means of Program Assessment

Respondents indicated how they assess whether their fellowships programs are meeting goals.

No program assessment	21.9%
Program self-review	70.1%
Surveys	33.9%
Benchmarking	29.5%
Focus groups	5.6%
Third-party evaluation	2.8%
Other program-assessment tools	6.8%

(No trend was discernible for *Other*.)

Data Collection

Respondents indicated whether they collect data on various measures of participation and success.

No fellowship data collected	4.3%
Number of students who receive awards	92.6%
Number of finalists for various awards	89.5%
Number of student applicants	89.1%
Number of students meeting with fellowships advisors	70.3%
Other direct measures of participation or success	14.8%

(Most common *Other* response was "Student Interaction.")

Learning and Development Outcomes

Respondents indicated whether they have created any learning and development outcomes for fellowship applicants.

Yes	23.7%
No	49.4%
Not yet but plan to create some	26.9%

Learning and Development Assessment—Means

Respondents indicated how they determine what students are learning from the application process.

No assessment of applicant learning	56.4%
Student surveys	34.9%
Essay reflections	13.5%
Student focus groups	4.4%
Third-party interviews	0.8%
Other means of learning assessment	9.5%

(Most common *Other* response was "Student Feedback.")

Learning and Development Assessment—Schedule

Respondents indicated when they evaluate what students are learning from the application process.

No assessment of applicant learning	56.6%
Annually	23.1%
After every fellowship application deadline	14.7%
Each term	4.8%
Other	5.6%

(No trend was discernible for *Other*.)

Assessment Reporting

Respondents indicated how they communicate assessment results.

No assessment results communicated	38.3%
In meetings with university	45.4%
In annual reports	50.2%
On the office website	11.6%
Through student interviews (in print, video, etc.)	9.6%
Other	4.4%

(No trend was discernible for *Other*.)

NAFA Resources

Respondents indicated what NAFA resources they use most frequently.

Listserv	91.9%
Conferences	73.9%
Workshops	36.2%
Website	40.8%
Informal mentorship	24.2%
Study tours	19.2%
Other	3.1%

(No trend was discernible for *Other*.)

NAFA Website Resources

Respondents indicated what NAFA website resources they use most frequently.

Resources Exchange	72.7%
Contacts	23.0%
Forums	26.3%
File sharing	28.2%
Other	5.3%

(No trend was discernible for *Other*.)

Supplemental Questions for Faculty Only

Tenure

Faculty respondents indicated whether they have tenure.

Yes	43.1%
No	56.9%

Faculty Assessment

Faculty respondents indicated who are assessed them for the purpose of their annual reviews.

Administrative unit to which fellowships report	53.9%
Home academic department	24.6%
Both administrative unit and academic department	21.5%

Salary Supplement

Faculty respondents indicated whether they receive a supplement to their base salary for working with fellowships advising.

No supplement	74.6%
1%–10% supplement	12.7%
11%–20% supplement	11.1%
21%–30% supplement	1.6%

Salary Retention

Faculty respondents indicated whether they would retain their base salary if they were not working with fellowships advising.

Yes	69.4%
No	30.7%

Release Time

Faculty respondents indicated whether they receive release time from teaching for their fellowship duties.

No release time	37.1%
1%–25% release	21.0%
26%–50% release	12.9%
51%–75% release	17.7%
76%–100% release	11.3%

Appendix

NATIONAL ASSOCIATION OF FELLOWSHIPS ADVISORS

Executive Board Members

Kyle Mox	President	Arizona State University
Craig Filar	Vice President	Florida State University
Jeff Wing	Treasurer	Virginia Commonwealth University
Robyn Curtis	Secretary	Clemson University
Andrus Ashoo	Board Member	University of Virginia
Monique Bourque	Board Member	Willamette University
Laura Clippard	Board Member	Middle Tennessee State University
Elizabeth Colucci	Board Member	University at Buffalo, SUNY
Brian Davidson	Board Member	Claremont McKenna College
Kim Germain	Board Member	University of Illinois at Chicago
Elizabeth Romig	Board Member	American University
Cindy Schaarschmidt	Board Member	University of Washington, Tacoma
Jayashree Shivamoggi	Board Member	Rollins College
Anne Wallen	Board Member	University of Kansas
John Mateja	Foundation Representative	Goldwater Scholarship Foundation
Lauren Tuckley	Communications Director	Georgetown University
John Richardson	Administrative Manager	NAFA

University and Foundation Members

ACIE-Critical Language
  Scholarship Program
Albion College
Allegheny College
Alma College
American Association for the
  Advancement of Science
American Association of
  University Women (AAUW)
American Friends of the Alexander
  von Humboldt Foundation
American Society For Engineering
  Education
American University
Amherst College
Appalachian State University
Arizona State University
Arkansas State University
Arkansas Tech University
Astronaut Scholarship Foundation
Auburn University
Augsburg College
Ball State University
Bard College
Barnard College
Barry Goldwater Scholarship
  Foundation
Baruch College, CUNY
Bates College
Baylor University
Benedictine College
Bennington College
Berklee College of Music
Binghamton University
Boise State University

Boston University
Bowdoin College
Bowling Green State University
Brandeis University
Bridgewater State University
Brigham Young University
Brooklyn College, CUNY
Brown University
Bryant University
Bryn Mawr College
Bucknell University
Buena Vista University
Butler University
California Polytechnic State
  University
California Polytechnic State
  University, Pomona
California Institute of Technology
California State University,
  East Bay
California State University,
  Los Angeles
California State University,
  Monterey Bay
Cambridge Trust
Carleton College
Carnegie Endowment for
  International Peace
Carnegie Mellon University
Carthage College
Case Western Reserve University
Central Michigan University
Centre College
Cerritos College
Chapman University

Christendom College

City College of New York—CUNY

Claremont McKenna College

Clark Atlanta University

Clark University

Clarkson University

Clemson University

Coe College

Colgate University

College of Charleston

College of New Jersey

St. John's University

College of Staten Island

College of the Holy Cross

College of William & Mary

College Track

Colorado College

Colorado School of Mines

Colorado State University

Columbia University

Columbus State University

Concordia College—Moorhead

Connecticut College

Cornell College

Cultural Vistas—Alfa Fellowship Program

DAAD German Academic Exchange Service

Dartmouth College

Davidson College

Delta College

Denison University

DePauw University

Dickinson College

Doane University

Drake University

Drexel University

Duke Kunshan University

Duke University

Duquesne University

Durham University

East Carolina University

Eastern Connecticut State University

Eastern Kentucky University

Eckerd College

Elizabethtown College

Elmhurst College

Elon University

Embry-Riddle Aeronautical University

Emmanuel College

Emory and Henry College

Emory University

Fairfield University

Fannie and John Hertz Foundation

Florida Atlantic University

Florida Gulf Coast University

Florida International University

Florida Southern College

Florida State University

Fordham University

Fort Hays State University

Franklin and Marshall College

Furman University

Gates Cambridge

George Mason University

George Washington University

Georgetown University

Georgia College and State University

Georgia Institute of Technology

Georgia State University
Gettysburg College
Grand Valley State University
Grinnell College
Gustavus Adolphus College
Hamilton College
Hampden-Sydney College
Harding University
Harvard University
Hastings College
Johns Hopkins University
Juniata College
Kalamazoo College
Kansas State University
Kean University
Kennesaw State University
Kent State University
Kentucky Wesleyan College
Kenyon College
King's College London
Knight-Hennessy Scholars
Knox College
Lafayette College
LaGuardia Community College,
    CUNY
Lamar University
Lawrence University
Le Moyne College
Lebanon Valley College
Lehigh University
Lehman College, CUNY
LeMoyne College
Lenoir-Rhyne University
Lewis & Clark College
Liberty University
Linfield College
Louisiana State University

Loyola Marymount University
Loyola University Chicago
Loyola University Maryland
Loyola University New Orleans
Lubbock Christian University
Luther College
Macalester College
Manhattan College
Marist College
Marshall Aid Commemoration
    Commission
Marshall University
Massachusetts College of Liberal
    Arts
Massachusetts Institute of
    Technology
McDaniel College
McKendree University
Mercer University
Mercyhurst University
Miami University
Michigan State University
Michigan Technological
    University
Middle Tennessee State University
Middlebury College
Middlebury Institute of
    International Studies
Minnesota State University,
    Mankato
Mississippi State University
Missouri University of Science and
    Technology
Mitchell Scholarship Program
Monmouth College
Montana State University
Montgomery College

Moravian College
Mount Holyoke College
Mount Saint Mary's University
Muhlenberg College
Murray State University
New College of Florida
New Jersey Institute of Technology
New Mexico State University
New York University
New York University of Abu
    Dhabi
New York University Shanghai
NIH Oxford-Cambridge Scholars
    Program
North Carolina A&T State
    University
North Carolina State University
Northeastern University
Northern Arizona University
Northern Illinois University
Northern Kentucky University
Northwestern University
Oakland University
Oberlin College
Occidental College
Ohio Northern University
Ohio State University
Ohio University
Oklahoma State University
Old Dominion University
Olin College of Engineering
Oregon State University
Pace University
Pacific Lutheran University
Pat Tillman Foundation
Paul & Daisy Soros Fellowships
    for New Americans

Penn State Behrend
Penn State University
Pepperdine University
Pitzer College
Pomona College
Portland State University
Prairie View A&M University
Pratt Institute
Princeton University
Providence College
Purdue University
Purdue University Northwest
Queen's University Belfast
Queens College, CUNY
Queens University of Charlotte
Quinnipiac University
Ramapo College of New Jersey
Rangel International Affairs
    Program
Reed College
Rensselaer Polytechnic Institute
Rhode Island School of Design
Rhodes College
Rice University
Roanoke College
Robert Bosch Foundation
    Fellowship Program
Robert Morris University
Rochester Institute of Technology
Rollins College
Roosevelt University
Rowan University
Royal Holloway, University of
    London
Rutgers University
Rutgers University—New
    Brunswick

Rutgers University—Camden
Saint Joseph's University
Salem State University
Salisbury University
San Diego State University
San Francisco State University
Santa Clara University
Sarah Lawrence College
Schwarzman Scholars
    Program, Tsinghua
    University
Scripps College
Seattle University
Seton Hall University
Siena College
Skidmore College
Slippery Rock University
Smith College
Southern Adventist University
Southern Utah University
Southwestern University
St. Catherine University
St. Edward's University
St. John's College, Annapolis
St. John's University
St. Lawrence University
St. Louis University
St. Norbert College
St. Olaf College
Stanford University
Stetson University
Stonehill College
Stony Brook University
SUNY Buffalo State
SUNY Cortland
SUNY Geneseo
SUNY New Paltz

SUNY Old Westbury
SUNY Oswego
SUNY Cortland
Susquehanna University
Swarthmore College
Syracuse University
Temple University
Tennessee Tech University
Texas A&M University
Texas A&M University-Kingsville
Texas State University
Texas Tech University
The Beinecke Scholarship
    Program
The Citadel
The Harry S. Truman Scholarship
    Foundation
The Honor Society of Phi Kappa
    Phi
The Morris K. Udall and
    Stewart L. Udall Foundation
The Posse Foundation
The Rhodes Trust
The Rotary Foundation of Rotary
    International
The Washington Center
The Winston Churchill
    Foundation of the US
Thiel College
Towson University
Trinity College
Truman State University
Tufts University
Tulane University
U.S. Air Force Academy
U.S. Coast Guard Academy
U.S. Department of State

U.S. Military Academy at West
  Point
U.S. Naval Academy
Union College
Union University
University at Albany, SUNY
University at Buffalo, SUNY
University College London
University of Alabama
University of Alabama at
  Birmingham
University of Alabama in
  Huntsville
University of Alaska Anchorage
University of Arizona
University of Arkansas
University of Arkansas at
  Pine Bluff
University of Bristol
University of California, Berkeley
University of California, Davis
University of California, Irvine
University of California,
  Los Angeles
University of California, Merced
University of California, Riverside
University of California,
  San Diego
University of California,
  Santa Barbara
University of Central Arkansas
University of Central Florida
University of Chicago
University of Cincinnati
University of Colorado at Boulder
University of Connecticut
University of Dallas

University of Dayton
University of Denver
University of East Anglia
University of Florida
University of Georgia
University of Glasgow
University of Houston
University of Idaho
University of Illinois at Chicago
University of Illinois at Springfield
University of Illinois at
  Urbana-Champaign
University of Indianapolis
University of Iowa
University of Kansas
University of Kansas Medical
  Center
University of Kentucky
University of Louisville
University of Lynchburg
University of Maine Orono
University of Manchester
University of Mary Washington
University of Maryland,
  Baltimore County
University of Maryland,
  College Park
University of Massachusetts
  Amherst
University of Massachusetts
  Boston
University of Massachusetts
  Lowell
University of Memphis
University of Miami
University of Michigan,
  Ann Arbor

University of Minnesota
University of Minnesota, Morris
University of Minnesota, Rochester
University of Mississippi
University of Missouri—Columbia
University of Missouri—Kansas City
University of Montana
University of Nebraska—Lincoln
University of Nebraska at Omaha
University of Nevada Las Vegas
University of Nevada, Reno
University of New Hampshire
University of New Mexico
University of North Alabama
University of North Carolina at Chapel Hill
University of North Carolina at Charlotte
University of North Carolina at Greensboro
University of North Carolina Wilmington
University of North Dakota
University of North Florida
University of North Georgia
University of North Texas
University of Northern Iowa
University of Notre Dame
University of Oklahoma
University of Oregon
University of Pennsylvania
University of Pittsburgh
University of Portland
University of Puget Sound
University of Rhode Island

University of Richmond
University of Rochester
University of Scranton
University of Sheffield
University of South Alabama
University of South Carolina
University of South Carolina Beaufort
University of South Dakota
University of South Florida
University of Southampton
University of Southern California
University of Southern Indiana
University of Southern Mississippi
University of St. Thomas
University of Sussex
University of Tennessee at Chattanooga
University of Tennessee, Knoxville
University of Texas at Dallas
University of Texas at San Antonio
University of Texas Rio Grande Valley
University of the Pacific
University of Toledo
University of Tulsa
University of Utah
University of Vermont
University of Virginia
University of Warwick
University of Washington
University of West Georgia
University of Wisconsin—Eau Claire
University of York
Ursinus College

Utah State University
Valparaiso University
Vanderbilt University
Vassar College
Victims of Pan Am Flight 103, Inc
Villanova University
Virginia Commonwealth
    University
Virginia Military Institute
Virginia Tech University
Wabash College
Wake Forest University
Walsh University
Washington and Lee University
Washington College
Washington State University
Washington University in
    St. Louis
Watson Foundation
Wellesley College
Wesleyan University
West Texas A&M University

West Virginia University
Western Carolina University
Western Kentucky University
Western Washington University
Westminster College
Wheaton College (MA)
Whitman College
Whittier College
Willamette University
Williams College
Winona State University
Winthrop University
Wofford College
Woodrow Wilson National
    Fellowship Foundation
Worcester Polytechnic Institute
    (WPI)
Xavier University of Louisiana
Yale University
Yale-NUS College
Yeshiva University
Young Harris College

Index

Page numbers followed by *f* indicate figures and *t* indicate tables.